HIS *Love*
NEVER QUITS

HIS *Love* NEVER QUITS

Finding Purpose Through Your Pain

CHERIE HILL

Waterfall
PRESS

Published by Waterfall Press, Grand Haven, MI
www.brilliancepublishing.com

Amazon, the Amazon logo, and Waterfall Press are trademarks of Amazon.com, Inc., or its affiliates.

ISBN-13: 9781477824726
ISBN-10: 1477824723

Cover design by Laura Klynstra
Interior design and composition by Greg Johnson/Textbook Perfect

Library of Congress Control Number: 2014936133

Permissions continued on page 117.

To my two precious boys,
Carson and Davis.

I love you both more than you will ever know.

It has been through the gift of your lives
that I have seen the face of God and
experienced His presence, power, and peace.

It is because of *God's perfect love for you* that
He taught me to trust Him—*no matter what.*

Contents

As for God, *his way is perfect.*

PSALM 18:30 (NIV)

1

Can God Be Trusted?

*L*ife has taken some unexpected turns. You've either decided to take detours in your life, or you've been forced into them... only to find yourself at a dead *end*. The twists and turns have distorted your sense of direction and you feel like you're spinning out of control. You've been striving to take the "high" road, but without warning you find yourself shoved off the road altogether, and you've landed in a ditch (the "valley").

It appears you're in the middle of nowhere. And when you need help the most... *there's not a soul in sight.*

If faith is supposed to be an insurance policy against the tragedies in life, it isn't paying off.

In a moment of solemn realization, you're surprised you've survived thus far. But in times like these, *there have been moments when you wish you hadn't.* The truth is, you're

calling out to God, but He doesn't seem to be answering. Desperation is draining you and you're exhausted from the "fight of faith." Doubt seems to be getting the best of you.

If God is at work, *you can't see it*. If God really loves you, *you can't feel it*. And if He doesn't show up in your circumstances, *it's the end of the road*. As the reality of the situation sets in, you can't help but wonder if God *really* cares. You reason, "He could have been there and *He wasn't*. He could have done something and *He didn't*." Looking back, your prayers even seem like cruel jokes...when you hoped for good, *evil came*; when you looked for light, *darkness came flooding in:*

> Yet, when I hoped for good, evil came; when I looked for light, then came darkness. The churning inside me never stops; days of suffering confront me.
> (JOB 30:26–27 NIV)

You realize that what you've been wrestling with aren't simple matters of faith, but feelings of abandonment and betrayal by a God who claims to love you. Your soul begins to cry out:

> How long, O LORD, must I call for help?
> But you do not listen! [. . .]
> I cry, but you do not come to save.
> (HABAKKUK 1:2 NLT)

As if things couldn't get worse, God remains silent and the emptiness intensifies. Why does God allow pain and suffering?

> *Though God seems silent He always hears,*
> *providing His peace that calms our fears.*
> *It's through our pain that we tend to shut God out,*
> *not realizing our sorrow and pain brings us into the quiet-*
> *ness where His still voice shouts.*
> —CHERIE HILL

Albeit true, we just wish God wouldn't shout so loud! Are we really that deaf? Evidently so:

> *They have ears but cannot hear.*
> (PSALM 115:6 NLT)

Yet as He shouts at us, why can't we see Him? Where is He when we need Him? He calls to us through the megaphone of pain, but when we come running, *we can't find Him*!

> *But if I go to the east, he is not there;*
> *if I go to the west, I do not find him.*
> *When he is at work in the north, I do not see him;*
> *when he turns south, I catch no glimpse of him.*
> (JOB 23:8–9 NIV)

Doubt steps into the picture once again, and the questions begin to spiral out of control:

Does He know what we're going through?
Does He understand our desperation?

Through the silence, there's a whisper in our spirit, and briefly we recall:

Even though Jesus was God's Son,
he learned obedience
from the things he suffered.
(HEBREWS 5:8 NLT)

For we do not have a High Priest who is unable to empathize with our weaknesses, but we have one who has been tempted in every way, just as we are—yet he did not sin.
(HEBREWS 4:15 NIV)

Our spirit is calmed as we realize that a deep desire is satisfied: We not only want a God who knows all about our pain, *we want a God who shares in it.*

He was despised and rejected by mankind,
a man of suffering,
*and **familiar with pain**.*
(ISAIAH 53:3 NIV)

Although we might argue that our situation is as painful as enduring the cross, our argument just simply doesn't hold water. Our *blood and water* have not been spilled out, literally. As we humble ourselves at the foot of the cross, in a brief moment of calm, we can't help but wonder, "*Does*

God know something I don't? Is it possible… that things look different from His perspective and He knows the bigger picture? Is it feasible that in my pain and suffering, He IS working all things for good and I just can't see it?" Maybe, *just maybe,* God knows what He's doing. In a moment of reckoning, we realize:

> "God allows in His wisdom what He could easily prevent in His power."
> —Graham Cooke

Even though that revelation is thought provoking and fairly "faith stretching"…knowing that God loves us and works "all things for good," *in the end, just doesn't seem to be enough.*

The begging question within our soul is, *"Can God be trusted?"* As we ponder the answer, we recall that God's ways are higher:

> For just as the heavens are higher than the earth, so my ways are higher than your ways and my thoughts higher than your thoughts.
> (Isaiah 55:9 NLT)

We're convinced that His thoughts are higher than our thoughts—as hard as we try, *we can't figure God out.* And His ways may be higher, *but they certainly don't seem better.* We made plans for our lives, but He's determining our steps *and taking us places we never wanted to go.*

*We can make our plans, but the LORD
determines our steps.*
(PROVERBS 16:9 NLT)

We find ourselves taking the very next step in front of us, only to find our feet knocked out from under us. How can we trust a God who is constantly bringing us to our knees in helpless desperation? We decide to take the journey of life with Him and He brings us to the edge of a cliff. We find ourselves at the edge, consumed with fear, and God seems to push us right off; we're helpless and hopeless and free-falling into the abyss of darkness. *What kind of loving God does this?* Evidently, one who's teaching us to *trust* Him.

*Indeed these are the mere edges of His ways,
and how small a whisper we hear of Him!*
(JOB 26:14 NKJV)

The word "trust" is an interesting word. Its root is from the word that means "to lie facedown on the ground." With that in mind, we're starting to get the picture . . . that's why we've fallen and are unable to get up. *It's all about trust.* And God is bringing us to a place where faith is no longer an option or a luxury—*it's a necessity.*

Don't for a second believe that trust is a passive state of attitude and mind. Trust is a dynamic, vital act of the soul by which we choose to take hold of the promises of God and cling to them, despite any adversity that seeks to overwhelm us. In our moment of reckoning, as difficult as it is, our suffering Savior versed words that cause our faith to deplete even more, as we realize we don't have the faith that *willingly, gladly, and trustingly* drinks of the cup of suffering that God has handed us:

> *"Shall I not drink from the cup of suffering*
> *the Father has given me?"*
> (JOHN 18:11 NLT)

Though it's not what we want to hear, Jesus exemplifies how we are to trust God. Surrendering everything to God is the highest form of faith, especially when it includes suffering.

> "This was a greater thing to say and do than calm the seas or raise the dead. Prophets and apostles could work wondrous miracles, but they could not always do and suffer the will of God. To do and suffer God's will is still the highest form of faith, the most sublime Christian achievement. To have the bright aspirations of a younger life forever blasted; to bear a daily burden never congenial and to see no relief; to be pinched by poverty when you only desire a competency for the good and comfort of loved ones; to be fettered by some incurable physical disability; to be stripped bare of loved ones until you stand alone to meet the shocks of life—to be able to say in such a school of discipline, 'Shall I not drink from the cup of suffering my Father has given me?'—this is faith at its highest and spiritual success at the crowning point. Great faith is exhibited not so much in ability to do as to suffer."
> —DR. CHARLES PARKHURST

We want to trust, we want to have faith that moves mountains, but we need to be sure that God will not allow anything to thwart His glory. We need to be assured that nothing will keep Him from giving us *good* things in life. We need to know that He's *in charge*—that nothing happens outside of His awareness. We need to be assured that *no one* and *nothing* can act outside of God's sovereign will or against it. Once again, we hear His voice whispering to our troubled minds:

> *I am God, and there is no other;*
> *I am God, and there is none like me.*
> *I make known the end from the beginning,*
> *from ancient times, what is still to come.*
> *I say, 'My purpose will stand, and I will do all that I please.'*
> (ISAIAH 46:9–10 NIV)

To us, our situation looks hopeless, but the place of hopelessness is where God can show Himself powerfully in our lives. What we find, as we wait on God to reveal His will, is that oftentimes *He only reveals Himself.*

In our continued suffering, our question of, "Where is God when I'm hurting?" turns to a question like, "Where is God when it doesn't stop?" And what we find is that God is at work in our lives…He never sleeps or slumbers (see Psalm 121:4)…through our hopelessness, He's drawing us near, preparing us to make a decision. Will we trust Him? Will we take Him at His word?

In times of desperation, we will do one of two things: run *from* God or run *to* Him. It's our choice. And if we'll trust Him while we're upon our knees, He will take us through a journey of faith that allows us to fully grasp how Romans 8:28 (NIV) reads into our life:

> *And we know that in all things God works for the good of those who love him, who have been called according to his purpose.*

In *job layoffs*, God works for the good.
In *divorce*, God works for the good.
In *pain and suffering*, God works for the good.
In *broken relationships*, God works for the good.
In *sickness*, God works for the good.
In *addictions*, God works for the good.
In *loss and grief*, God works for the good.

In your hour of need, God is going to show you that *He is all you need.* He's the Redeemer. It may be Saturday, but God is a God of Sundays—resurrection days. When you're trusting in God, you're trusting in the power that raises the dead...*He may be only moments from rolling your stone away.* He wants us to trust Him on Saturday...*He's looking for our faith.*

> *For the eyes of the LORD range throughout the earth*
> *to strengthen those whose*
> *hearts are fully committed to him.*
> (2 CHRONICLES 16:9 NIV)

Now, it *may not* look like Sunday is coming... trusting God is never easy, *but it makes all things possible.* You see, God loves to do the impossible, so if you're at the edge, *upon your knees* in desperation, God's got you right where He wants you. *He's brought you to this very place.* (Unfortunately, some of us just have farther to go to get there.)

He led the Israelites to the Red Sea—
He's led you to yours.

God allowed Daniel to be thrown into a den of lions to be devoured—*He's done the same with you.*

He gave David the opportunity to defeat a giant—*He's giving you the chance as well.*

He permitted Shadrach, Meshach, and Abednego to step into a fiery furnace, but He met them there... *He'll meet you in your furnace of affliction.* He gave Peter the opportunity to walk on water—*He's calling you upon it too. But you'll have to trust Him.* That's what He's after... your trust in Him. He's after your heart...

the one that's breaking.

And He needs you to make a decision... sometimes many times a day, hour, or minute—to trust Him. It's your choice... *He leaves the decision to you.* Want to see His track record? Check out the Old and New Testaments. Not a SINGLE person regretted trusting God... *but the whole Bible is filled with the sorrows of those who decided not to.*

Trusting God is only possible if you make a decision—a decision to "take His word for it." God's word is His promises to you...and you can bet your life on every single one of them.

*"Anyone who believes in him
will never be put to shame."*
(ROMANS 10:11 NIV)

You can make the decision to simply trust God and then watch Him prove Himself faithful, or He'll bring you to a place of needing to trust Him. And most of the time, the walk of faith entails both ways. At the end of all hope, *when you're being tested beyond measure,* when you are no longer able to trust anyone BUT God...there's a way of escape, *but it isn't the way you probably envisioned.*

*The temptations in your life are no different
from what others experience. And God is faithful.
He will not allow the temptation to be more than
you can stand. When you are tempted, he will
show you a way out so that you can endure.*
(1 CORINTHIANS 10:13 NLT)

The way out! That's what we're hoping for. *But God's ways aren't our ways.* He's taking us a different route...*right through the valley of adversity.* He's bringing us to the end of our will *so that we will embrace His.* And unexpectedly, we get a glimpse of just *one* of the ways of God. He brings us into brokenness *so that He can make us whole.*

Indeed we felt we had received the sentence of death.
But this happened that we might
not rely on ourselves,
but on God, who raises the dead.
(2 CORINTHIANS 1:9 NIV)

What we find, at the point of no return, is that the only way out is *through... and the only way through is by trusting God.* As if life were not difficult enough, that somber revelation is not in the least bit encouraging. In fact, on the surface of it, that means *things will probably get worse.* Can we really trust God when adversity consumes our life with pain? Does He really come to the rescue of those who seek Him? Does He, as His word says, deliver those who call upon Him in the day of trouble (see Psalm 50:15)?

You're not the first to ask such pertinent questions in the matters of faith, and you won't be the last. Do these words seem eerily familiar at all?

When I was in deep trouble, I searched for the Lord. All night long I pray, with hands lifted toward heaven, pleading. There can be no joy for me until he acts. I think of God, and I moan, overwhelmed with longing for his help. You don't let me sleep. I am too distressed even to pray! I think of the good old days, long since ended, when my nights were filled with joyful songs. I search my soul and think about the difference now. Has the Lord rejected me forever? Will he never again show me favor? Is his unfailing love gone forever? Have his promises permanently failed? Has God forgotten to be kind? Has he

slammed the door on his compassion? And I said, "This is my fate, the blessings Most High have changed to hatred."
(PSALM 77:2–10 NLT)

As we struggle in our faith, doubt steps into the conversation and asks the begging question, "Can God be trusted?"

He's glad you asked.

It's a Choice

You need to make a choice—God's way or your way. And God has spoken:

"As for God, his way is perfect."
(PSALM 18:30 NIV)

You see, your life is your vote... you're either for Him or against Him (see Luke 11:12). You either believe Him *or you don't.* You either live your life trusting Him *or you call Him a liar.* Though that's a rather harsh statement, it's reality. You *must* cast your vote... everyone must—believers and unbelievers alike. Each and every day, we cast our vote.

God is not human, that he should lie, not a human being, that he should change his mind. Does he speak and then not act? Does he promise and not fulfill?
(NUMBERS 23:19 NIV)

It's *not* about believing in Him... *even demons believe.*

You believe there is one God. Good!
Even the demons believe that—
and shudder.

(JAMES 2:19 NIV)

Believing God is a different matter altogether. It's trusting God. It's having faith in whom He says He is through His word. Just as faith comes from hearing the word of God (see Romans 10:17), trust is based upon our faith...it's stepping out in faith and being assured that God is true to His word. We believe we have faith, we trust God and take Him at His word, but until we're forced to rely on the faith we think we have, our faith is never reliable and proven.

The truth is, in moments of doubt, all we need to do is stop and take a deep breath, look around us, and quite frankly, *observe the obvious.*

The evidence that God exists is so overwhelming that it is simply senseless to spend any amount of time thinking otherwise.

Francis Chan urges us to just stop and think:

"Right now you're standing on this giant ball that's spinning at a thousand miles an hour! And while it's spinning, it's flying around the sun at 67,000 miles an hour! That's crazy!"

—FRANCIS CHAN, "STOP AND THINK"

If God can keep the universe in motion, surely we can trust Him with our lives. Yet we doubt the One who placed each star in the sky. In Psalm 8:3–4 (NIV) we reflect:

When I consider your heavens, the work of your fingers, the moon and the stars, which you have set in place, what is mankind that you are mindful of them, human beings that you care for them?

God is a God of details . . . and He knows every detail of your life. Never doubt that He does:

And the very hairs on your head are all numbered. So don't be afraid; you are more valuable to God than a whole flock of sparrows.
(LUKE 12:7 NLT)

(P.S. If you don't have hairs on your head, God knows that too!)

But doubt comes knocking regularly, doesn't it! Rest assured, God's word holds true once more. He uses ALL things for good . . . *even doubt.*

"If we never encounter doubt, we'll never truly grasp faith. Doubt is our opportunity to live by the faith we profess."
—CHERIE HILL

Know that it's okay to doubt. If you're not willing to entertain doubt and let doubt make its case, your faith may never grow and become the footbridge that is needed to cross your chasm.

It's okay to have doubt in the midst of your faith, but allowing doubt to rule in your life is, as John Ortberg puts it in his book, *Faith and Doubt, "like jumping off a diving board and trying to put off actually entering into the water."*

You put yourself in an impossible situation. Sooner or later, you need to trust that the water is there and simply jump in. You have to *believe* something before you *doubt* anything, so give yourself a break and realize that *every* saint doubts. Your belief in God is the first step, but it's ultimately trusting Him that not only puts you in the water, *but causes you to walk upon it.*

But *it's your choice.* And *not* choosing is its own choice. Trusting God is not a decision you make once. It's a choice that must be made countless times a day. The decision will sometimes be small, at other times, *life changing.* Either way, the choice comes down to whether or not you believe that God is trustworthy.

Peter had a chance to trust God. (Note: The other disciples stayed in the boat. Peter took a risk—He chose to trust, *even through his doubts.*) Jesus called to Peter as He walked upon the water:

"*Lord, if it is you,*" Peter replied, "*tell me to come to you on the water.*" "*Come,*" He said. Then Peter got down out of the boat, walked on the water, and came toward Jesus. But when he saw the wind, he was afraid and, beginning to sink, cried out, "*Lord, save me!*" Immediately Jesus reached out His hand and caught him. "*You of little faith,*" He said,

"why did you doubt?"

One thing that stands out in this story is that the disciples had "gone ahead" of Jesus. We're not sure if that was by their choice or Jesus's, but we know that we tend to go ahead of God from time to time. (Okay, more often than not.) Yet what's even more remarkable about this story is that although the disciples thought they were "ahead" of Him, Jesus came walking to them. It seems we're NEVER ahead of God. We're no different from Peter... we WANT to believe, *but our circumstances get the best of us.*

The winds of adversity begin to instill fear in our hearts and we take our eyes off Jesus. Trusting in God requires taking risks and trusting in Christ-centered help. *Mature faith will never develop in shallow water.*

There's another place where there was a choice that had to do with water... it was a healing at a pool. The pool of water had been known to cure people. The waters were said to make the blind to see and the lame to walk, yet there was one man who had been an invalid sitting by the pool for thirty-eight years. (Wow, that's a long time, *yet we, too, sit on this side of faith allowing doubt to get the best of us.*) When Jesus saw him, He asked him, "*Do you want to get well?*" (A choice had to be made.) What seemed like a ridiculous question revealed the choice God gives us in the obvious situations of life... we must want His help. The man's response is even more shocking, as he is before the Son of God... making up excuses! (Haven't we done the same?) "*Sir,*" the invalid replied, "*I have no one to help me into the pool when the water is stirred. While I am trying to get in, someone else goes down ahead of me.*" (We mock his excuse—"How absurd is that!" Yet our excuses are no better.) Then Jesus said to him, "*Get up! Pick up your mat*

and walk!" At once the man was cured; he picked up his mat and walked. (Did you catch that? AT ONCE!)

Listen, don't wait for Jesus to come to you. Go to Him. Don't expect a divine sign from heaven or a feeling within your soul before you choose to trust God. Rest assured, in times of hopelessness, those things will never occur. There may not be anyone there to *"help you into the healing pool when the water is stirred."* Most often you're going to have to encourage yourself in the Lord. You're going to have to "Get up!" and walk forward in faith . . . trusting that God is true to His word.

> David encouraged himself
> in the LORD his God.
> (1 SAMUEL 30:6 KJV)

Know that once you take a step of faith, you'll be met with winds of adversity that instill fear in your heart; there'll be doubts that try to keep you from taking another step toward God—you'll come face-to-face with the enemy, the devil. An old southern preacher once said,

> "If you don't come face-to-face with the devil
> sometimes, then you must be going the same
> direction he is."

Make sure you're not moving in the same direction as the devil. Don't be afraid to face him. If God is for you, who would dare be against you (see Romans 8:31)? Know that each obstacle you face is part of the enemy's strategy, *but tools in the hands of God.* As hard as it is to accept, God calls the shots. And yes, He allows "good" as well as "bad."

> *When times are good, be happy; but when times are bad, consider this: God has made the one as well as the other.*
> (ECCLESIASTES 7:14 NIV)

> *"Should we accept only good things from the hand of God and never anything bad?"*
> (JOB 2:10 NLT)

The sooner we realize that God is God and we're not, the better off we'll be. (His throne isn't big enough for the two of you.) If we choose to sit upon our own throne, running our own kingdom, *He'll let us.* But He urges us to trust Him. He pleads His case within the Bible and urges us to choose "life"—*His way.*

> *This day I call heaven and earth as witnesses against you that **I have set before you life and death, blessings and curses. Now choose life**, so that you and your children may live.*
> (DEUTERONOMY 30:19 NIV)

God makes it clear: it's our choice. And the choice is vital. There is nothing more critical than life and death, nothing *more* desirable on earth than blessings and nothing *less* desirable than curses. How much easier can the choice be?

The question is, "Will we do it God's way *or our own?*" We are all earthen vessels, but whether or not we claim to be the captain of the ship is a vital part of whether we arrive safely at our destination, sink at sea, or end up lost in the vast ocean for eternity.

As the story goes, there was a ship sailing through black water on a black night… the seaman on watch saw a light ahead. He reported to the captain, who immediately ordered the following message sent:

"Request that you alter your course 10 degrees south."

The reply: *"Request that you alter your course 10 degrees north."*

The captain, now angry, sent another message, a little more terse than the first: *"Request you alter your course 10 degrees south. I am the captain."*

The reply: *"Request you alter your course 10 degrees north. I am a third-class seaman."*

This time, the captain became furious: *"Request you alter your course 10 degrees south. I am a battleship."*

The reply: *"Request you alter your course 10 degrees north. I am a lighthouse. It's up to you."*

It's up to you. The choice is yours. Jesus is the lighthouse in our lives. The adversities in our lives are avenues that God uses to direct us to Himself, once again. God has made the way for us:

> I am **the way**
> and the truth and the life.
> (JOHN 14:6 NIV)

In times of darkness, don't doubt what God has shown you in the light. It all comes down to whether or not we trust God. And our question, "Can God be trusted?" is only answered by yet another question, *"Is God REALLY sovereign?"* Our faith hinges on our answer to that *one* question. And *our answer changes everything.*

Who's in Charge?

There's no such thing as God being almost sovereign. He either is or He isn't. And if He isn't, then He can't be trusted.

You see, God is real, whether we believe He is or not. Our disbelief doesn't erase His existence—just as our lack of faith and trust in Him doesn't nullify His faithfulness.

What if some were unfaithful?
Will their unfaithfulness nullify God's faithfulness?
(ROMANS 3:3 NIV)

If we are faithless,
he remains faithful,
for he cannot disown himself.
(2 TIMOTHY 2:13 NIV)

You may be at a place in which you're not even sure God exists, much less at a point of trusting in His sovereignty; you may need to take a step back and understand *why* it is you should believe.

Note: if you've never trusted Jesus as your Savior and you're exhausted from the trials of life and going your own way, you can come to Him now. (He's always waiting.) Without Christ, your suffering is meaningless misery. But if you'll let Him take control of your life, becoming Lord and Savior, He'll walk with you through every difficulty and give you unimaginable peace and joy, even in the midst of pain. If you would like to accept His offer of salvation, you can pray:

> *Lord Jesus, I believe you are truly the Son of God. I confess that I have sinned against You in thought, word, and deed. Please forgive me for all of my wrongdoings and let me now live in relationship with You going forward. I receive You as my personal Savior, accepting the work You accomplished on the cross to save me from my sins. Fill me with the Holy Spirit so that I might follow You all the days of my life. Amen.*

Once you've prayed that prayer, seek after Jesus with all that you are. Meditate on His word day and night. Grab hold of God and *never let go*. God loves you with an unfailing love.

The only way to trust God *is to know Him*. And knowing God is the key to finding peace and purpose in a life that can seem incredibly *overwhelming* on some days and absolutely *meaningless* on others. In His great love for us, He says that if we'll seek Him, we'll find Him . . . *if we seek Him with all of our heart.* And what we'll find is that ironically, His existence, His sovereignty, and His power and providence are *less about faith and more about facts.*

> You will seek me
> and find me when you seek me
> with all your heart.
> (JEREMIAH 29:13 NIV)

Although it may *seem* like it, God *isn't hiding from you.* He's not avoiding the tough questions or the awkward situations—

He's *always* waiting for you to come to Him.

> So the LORD must wait for you to come to him
> so he can show you his love and compassion.
> For the LORD is a faithful God.
> Blessed are those who wait for his help.
> (ISAIAH 30:18 NLT)

God waits for you to come to Him. He longs to pour out His love upon you and bring light into your darkness. But He loves you more than that...in His sovereignty, He knows that through this journey of life you will need to trust Him for everything, in order for you to experience peace and joy while on this earth. So He's allowed, *in His wisdom,* your situation of desperation. It's an opportunity for God to teach you something deeper about Himself. He has brought you to your knees so that you have nowhere to look *but up.* He has a habit of allowing us to dig holes so deep that we

can't get out without His help. *It's by design.* God is teaching us to trust. The paradox of the Christian faith walk is that *the strongest Christian is the weakest Christian.*

> *That is why, for Christ's sake,*
> *I delight in weaknesses, in insults, in hardships,*
> *in persecutions, in difficulties.*
> *For when I am weak, then I am strong.*
> (2 CORINTHIANS 12:10 NIV)
>
> *The weakness of God is stronger than human strength.*
> (1 CORINTHIANS 1:25 NIV)

But how do we trust God? How can we be sure of His promises? In order to trust God, we need to know Him. And in order to know Him...*we must listen to His voice.* And His voice is heard through His word.

> *My suffering was good for me,*
> *for it taught me to pay attention to your decrees.*
> (PSALM 119:71 NLT)

If we are to trust God, then it is crucial that we have confidence in His sovereignty in all that affects us. If there is a single event in all of the universe that can occur outside of God's sovereign control, then God can't be trusted. If you believe in a world of pure chance, what difference would it make if a plane crashes in a random city and yours makes it safely to its destination? But if you believe in a world that is ruled by a powerful, loving, and gracious God who cares for you at all times, then that belief makes an incredible difference.

We must be absolutely convinced that God's love is perfect and His wisdom infinite. Our trust in God cannot be based upon someone else's experience, but upon what God has told us about Himself in His word. We want to see God at work in *our* lives, yet we fail to realize that His hand is only visible to eyes of faith. And faith doesn't walk by sight.

"Faith is to believe what we do not see, and the reward of this faith is to see what we believe."
—ST. AUGUSTINE

We have to receive God by faith—by faith in His Son, Jesus Christ. When you learn to trust God, you don't have to see anything. You just know with all certainty that He's there:

There was a little boy who was out flying a kite. It was a fine day for kite flying; the wind was brisk and large billowy clouds were blowing across the sky. The kite went up and up until it was entirely hidden by the clouds. "What are you doing?" a man asked the little boy. "I'm flying a kite," he replied. "Flying a kite, are you?" the man asked. "How can you be sure? You can't see your kite." "No," said the boy, "I can't see it, but every little while I feel a tug, so I know for sure that it's there!"

Despite all appearances, we must trust God through our faith in His revealed word. His word is vital to our survival . . . it's what lights our path:

Your word is a lamp for my feet, a light on my path.
(PSALM 119:105 NIV)

We want to know His ways...*they're not hidden*—they're revealed through His word. As we seek Him and His voice through His word, we get a glimpse of God's ways—how He thinks and how He acts. He's told us that we need His word just as we need bread for our physical bodies:

"Man shall not live on bread alone, but on every word that comes from the mouth of God."
(MATTHEW 4:4 NIV)

God's word is straight from His mouth. His word was written to teach us:

Such things were written in the Scriptures long ago to teach us. And the Scriptures give us hope and encouragement as we wait patiently for God's promises to be fulfilled.
(ROMANS 15:4 NLT)

God's ways are revealed through His word. He loves you enough to speak to you—*to tell you the truth*. And through His words, we learn that He is sovereign—the Scriptures give proof throughout history that He is.

The Facts of Faith

God's word, the Bible, is the most unique book ever written. It is the bestselling book of all time for over two thousand years. That alone is astounding. Unique to the Bible is the foretelling of more than twenty-five hundred prophecies, of which approximately two thousand have already been fulfilled. (The remaining five hundred reach into the future and are yet to unfold.) You can find more astounding facts where faith meets science at: http://www.reasons.org.

If you're a numbers person, you can make an attempt to digest that the probability of any one of these prophecies having been fulfilled by chance is less than one in ten, conservatively. The more intriguing part is that the prophecies are for the most part independent of one another, so the odds for these being fulfilled by chance without error is less than 1 in 10^{2000}. (That's one with two thousand zeroes behind it! Facts found at reasons.org.)

Although others have partially predicted events over time, God specifically states in Deuteronomy 18:21–22 that He does not make even the SLIGHTEST error in His predictions. With God, there is NO room for error. These are facts . . . *not faith*.

For more than two thousand years, the Bible has been scrutinized more than any other book on earth. *No one* has been able to disprove its authenticity. Just the mere fact that it has survived such harsh critics should alert us to its supernatural quality. In a world of such abundant evil and cynicism, the Bible should have been dismantled a LONG time ago.

When you break down the Bible, its reliability must be tested just as any other ancient document. In order to study the Bible's reliability, historians have studied the number of existing manuscripts and the dating of those manuscripts. For starters, there are more than 5,300 Greek manuscripts of the New Testament that date from between 40 and 100 AD. If you include the manuscripts of the New Testament in Latin and earlier versions, the total number of manuscripts of the New Testament reaches more than twenty-four thousand. These are HISTORICAL documents, authenticated. Historians, not Christians, have proven it. The Bible is reliable. *And that changes everything.*

> *Heaven and earth will pass away, but my words will never pass away.*
> (MATTHEW 24:35 NIV)

For most, it's not the reliability of the Bible's documents that are the problem . . . it's the "supernatural" side of things that causes people not to believe. The bottom line: no matter how hard you try, you can't argue with God.

If you just go with the basics of the Bible, if you just think about it in a commonsense way, why would the writers of the greatest book in history acknowledge such dreadful sins and doubt in God? Why would God allow this to be written in His book? Why wouldn't you, as an author, paint a more rosy picture of yourself? Instead, God reveals the good, the bad, and the ugly. He reveals truth. He reveals His mercy and He assures His wrath. He sheds light on the trials of the greatest saints to ever walk the earth.

He shows their vulnerability, their fears, and their atrocious failures. He shows how He works in the lives of those who hate Him and how He gives grace to those who should never deserve it. He takes a man who murders Christians and makes him into an apostle who changes the course of the Christian faith forever. The apostle Paul, by his own admission, was the worst of sinners. Yet God reached down, made him blind, and then made him REALLY see.

You can look at every single documented event in the Bible and see that God is speaking to us. He's showing us things about Himself and ourselves. He has proven throughout history that He is absolutely trustworthy. Time and time again, He's shown that His grace prevails. Even when he was on the cross, the criminal who hung beside Jesus acknowledged his sin and laid his soul before God's mercy. The message: it's never too late to believe... *it's never too late to turn to God and trust Him.* His mercies never fail (see Lamentations 3:22).

In the face of all that you must go through in life... with all that you choose to believe in this life, why not take a risk and just make the choice to believe God... to take Him at His word? So many get to this point of decision, yet can't step forward... the reason... ***pride.***

Surrender

You may think you are going through trials and tragedies that are insurmountable, but none of them would compare to God abandoning you to yourself. Nothing would be more catastrophic than God allowing us to go our own way with no hope of turning back to Him. His love sees past our pride and *offers grace at every turn.* God knows that our pride keeps us from understanding our desperate natural condition. The truth is: we're corrupt in every facet of our character. But though we're broken, we can be fixed. God loves us too much to leave us as we are. So when we come to Him, when we abandon all else, we encounter a divine exchange: We surrender this life—God gives us TRUE life. Seems like a no-brainer, don't you think?

> *Then Jesus said to his disciples, "Whoever wants to be my disciple must deny themselves and take up their cross and follow me. For whoever wants to save their life will lose it, but whoever loses their life for me will find it. What good will it be for someone to gain the whole world, yet forfeit their soul? Or what can anyone give in exchange for their soul?"*
> (MATTHEW 16:24–26 NIV)

Forfeiting your soul—that's a depressing and defeating thought. But people do it every day—they forfeit their souls to addictions, hopelessness, fear, and despair. Maybe you've done it. If you have, *there's still hope.* As long as you're alive, you can be Jesus's disciple. All you have to do is *surrender.*

The great misconception is that God loves us just as we are. That's true and not true. The truth is, *He loves us too much to leave us as we are.* He's not going to leave us *where* He found us or *how* He found us if we surrender ourselves into His care. Truly, we must die to self. Why? Because all too often, our pride gets the best of us—we seem to think we're better than God. *We pick apart His plan and question His purposes.* In times of deep despair, *we dethrone Him through our doubt and find Him a failure through our fears.* We cling to what we know, see, and feel, and then declare that God just isn't there. We trust ourselves instead of God. And that...is the greatest tragedy. But God is greater than our sin...He's greater than our pride.

If we'll surrender, laying down our lives, and abandoning ourselves to Him, He'll go to work. In your surrender, His light will slowly but surely pierce the darkness you've been walking in. He'll reach down and save you. And then He'll take your brokenness and put you back together better than before. You can't make all your wrongs right, but God can. You can't change your heart's desires, but God will (see Ezekiel 36:26). You can't walk through your valley in your own strength, ***but you can do it in His.***

With all that God promises to do in exchange for surrendering our pride—which destroys our lives anyway—why wouldn't we run to Him in helpless abandon? Why

wouldn't we turn to Him and trust Him? It's for one reason alone: *we don't understand the depths of His love.*

Crazy Love

There's something you need to know about God before you trust Him...His love is CRAZY. In fact, His love makes *no sense at all.* Don't try and understand God's love—*just receive it.*

God's love not only abounds, it proliferates. It is unfailing and overflowing. His love is excessive and beyond measure. Yet when we're facing evil and suffering, we interpret our circumstances to mean that God doesn't love us after all. In fact, we're disappointed beyond words that His love for us doesn't exempt us from our pain and suffering. Isn't faith supposed to be our insurance policy against pain and suffering? If God loves us, why does He allow us to suffer? In the face of such difficult questions, and with the appearance that God is dodging them all, He speaks volumes through His word once more. After God revealed his name to Moses:

> And he passed in front of Moses, proclaiming,
> "The LORD, the LORD, the **compassionate**
> **and gracious** God, slow to anger,
> **abounding in love and faithfulness**,
> maintaining love to thousands,
> and forgiving wickedness, rebellion and sin."
> (EXODUS 34:6–7 NIV)

The love we know and experience here on earth sets us up for failure in our relationship with God. Superficial love does not withstand the test of time or trials of life. God doesn't love us on our terms, *but His.*

> The LORD's unfailing love surrounds
> the man who trusts in him.
> (PSALM 32:10 NIV)

> Have mercy on me, O God,
> according to your unfailing love.
> (PSALM 51:1 NIV)

Grasping the truth of God's love is the secret to a victorious life. God's love conquers all. No matter what you face, no matter the depths of your sin, God's love overcomes them all—not because of what you've done, but because of what He did…it's all about the cross…His love and mercy poured out WHILE we were still sinners. You can't gain God's love and you can't lose it. *It's crazy.* Hold on to truth and never let go. God's love will set you free and *keep* you free.

> This is love: not that we loved God,
> but that He loved us and sent His Son
> as an atoning sacrifice for our sins.
> We love Him because He **first** loved us.
> (1 JOHN 4:10 NIV, 19 NKJV)

To know God is to know that God's love remains even through our trials and temptations, through our joys and

pains, and through our *faith and doubt.* We must dwell in God's love and know that even though He is loving, He is holy...and holiness demands justice.

God is love, but He is not *only* love. We can't be fooled: God's love in the New Testament does not eclipse His holiness. If we think that God only loves and does not hate, then you'd think He'd only call upon us to love...*but He doesn't.* He commands, "*Hate evil, love good*" (see Amos 5:15 NIV). God is clear in the Psalms when He declares He "*is angry with the wicked every day*" (Psalm 7:11 NLT). To look at life through the eyes of God is to love good and hate evil. Our God of love is also a God of wrath (see Romans 1:18).

It was the same Jesus who spoke words of compassionate love and forgiveness who also spoke some of the harshest words of condemnation. Jesus spoke more about hell than anyone else in the Bible. His infinite love required Him to condemn and to call for repentance. Whom the Lord loves, He also disciplines; He punishes those whom He calls His children. So we can't be tempted to believe that just because we're being punished for our sins, or we're enduring the suffering caused by another's sins, God doesn't love us. He will love us *through* it. He'll use it all to draw us nearer to Him.

> *"Is not Israel still my son, my darling child?" says the* LORD.
> *"I often have to punish him, but I still love him. That's why I long for him and surely I will have mercy on him."*
> (JEREMIAH 31:20 NLT)

*"I have loved you my people, with an everlasting love.
With unfailing love I have drawn you to myself."*
(JEREMIAH 31:3 NLT)

His love, in its perfection, corrects and bandages us.
Though His hand may strike us, it also heals (see John
5:17–27). Though troubles come, *His love prevails.*

"His love never quits."
(PSALM 136:20 NIV)

The knowledge of God's love for you is the founda-
tional truth upon which all other truths are built. You can't
go forward in faith, you can't understand God's ways, until
you understand His love.

*Then Christ will **make his home in your hearts** as you
trust in him. Your roots will grow down into God's love
and keep you strong. And may you have the power to
understand, as all God's people should, how wide, how
long, how high, and how deep his love is. May you experience the love of Christ, though it is too great to understand
fully. **Then you will be made complete with all the fullness of life and power that comes from God.***
(EPHESIANS 3:17–19 NLT)

Did you catch that? He'll make a home in your heart.
The moment you fully accept God's love for you, something's about to happen: *He's about to make your heart His
home.* He's about to go to work. And all the construction is
going to seem chaotic—it's going to be painful.

As He oversees your circumstances, He's about to go to work on you. As you're trusting God, accepting His love, and pressing forward in faith, the chaos shouldn't be confused with the transforming works of God's hands. Although He destroys, He rebuilds. He's got the blueprints for your life...and *there's some work that needs to be done.* When you're trusting God, you're always a *"work in progress."*

2

Work in Progress

*I*f God says He never sleeps or slumbers (see Psalm 121:4), *we'd like to see proof of it.* In our trials we're not convinced that He's working *at all.* If He were, wouldn't our problems be solved? Why are we waiting around, seemingly wasting time? *Why is God silent when He should speak?* Is He just too busy with the rest of the universe? We can almost hear the automated response, *"Thank you for calling...your call will be answered in the order it was received...you are number 5,879,230,621...thank you for your patience...God will be with you momentarily."*

As we're put on hold, our despair has us grasping for hope amid complete hopelessness and holding on to our faith *with little* evidence that God will *ever* answer. Our words mimic our Savior's:

> *"Eli, Eli, lama sabachthani?"*
> *("My God, my God, why have you forsaken me?")*
> (MATTHEW 27:46 NIV)

And all of heaven is silent.

In perhaps the saddest two lines ever documented in history, Jesus shared in our feelings of abandonment. In this moment of agony, where He endured the suffering that was due *us*, He was separated for the first time from Almighty God—He endured the punishment for our sins. But God was at work. God had a plan. His ways are *always* higher. And if we'll trust Him, we'll never be disappointed.

> *Those who hope in me*
> *will not be disappointed.*
> (ISAIAH 49:23 NIV)

But as Jesus hung on His cross and we're crumbling beneath the weight of ours, God is silent. *It's His silence that is our greatest test of faith.* But in these moments of silence, God is at work. He's building our faith by threatening to destroy it. His delays are not His denials and *His silence is not His solution.*

Here's the thing: sometimes we wish God would show up with such intensity that His reality and power would be *overwhelmingly* evident. We want to see Him rip open heaven, reveal Himself, and then take His place among us here on earth. Quite frankly, *we'd like a little help down here!* Is that too much to ask? We want to see His hands laid upon the sick and witness miraculous healings. We'd like to see Him rise in the midst of a hurricane and cause the storm to cease. After all, *He used to show up that way.* In the Old

Testament, He showed up in ways with dramatic signs and wonders... *why can't He do that now?* In our questioning, as we try to go ahead of God, we find He's always one step ahead of us:

> *"Unless you people see signs and wonders," Jesus told him, "You will never believe."*
> (JOHN 4:48 NIV)

We think we've got Him stumped on this one. Now we've got God cornered with a question that He can't *satisfyingly* answer. If He's at work...

Where are the miracles?

God's answer takes us back to the Israelites. They were no different from us. They had a pattern in their life, and so do we—unbelief... *lack of trust in God.* The truth is we don't want to walk by faith... *we pray for our faith to take sight.* Yet God knows that seeing miracles doesn't build our relationship with Him. The proof is in the Old *and* New Testament. God answers our question... *it's just not what we wanted to hear.*

If we go back to the day of Moses when he was standing at the edge of the Red Sea with somewhere between two and three million Israelites needing to cross... and an Egyptian army encroaching, ready to slaughter them all... what had God done up to this point? *Miracles.* God had sent ten plagues upon the Egyptians—the last two being *especially* severe. God had rescued them out of slavery. Yet as they stood at the Red Sea, fear got the best of them and they began to cry out to God in anger. They declared it would have been better for them to have stayed in Egypt. But God stepped up to the plate, *despite their lack of faith,* and parted the Red Sea. He is faithful, *even when we're not.*

So God continued to lead them, yet He took them into a place of complete and utter helplessness—the wilderness. God took them into a situation that was out of their control. They had no control over their survival in the desolate desert where there was no food or water. They had no compass or maps—*they literally had NO IDEA where they were going.*

Though the situation didn't look good, God manifested Himself in a cloud in the daytime and a pillar of fire at night that they followed...and when it stopped, they rested (see Exodus 13:21–22, Numbers 9:34–36).

As they traveled, their need for food and water became intense. So God, hearing their murmurings, gave them water and bread. Not for just one day...for FORTY years (see Joshua 5:12). He made water come out of a ROCK! As if that were not enough, God supernaturally protected them from enemies in battle (see Exodus 17). Surely these miracles were enough to convince them of God's provision. Not quite. The Israelites grew weary and began to rebel against God. His *provisions* weren't meeting up to their *expectations.* It appears that mighty acts of God are not quite enough to convince us, going forward in life, that God is there and that He cares.

Yet God was at work. He had brought them into such desperation so that they might realize their need for Him and so that they had the opportunity to see His miraculous power at work in their lives. He took them into places that were completely beyond their control so that they might grow in faith...so that their faith would be unwavering. He wanted them to be a people that would trust Him completely, giving Him full control over every aspect of their lives, so that they would be a testimony to His love, mercy, and grace. *But that's not what happened. Most of them died* in the desert...for *lack of trust* in a God who had spoken to them, answered prayers, directed their every step, and continually performed miracles. (Something to think about.) That will NOT be me!

As if this example were not enough, God humbles us by bringing up the New Testament. God came down to earth. He stepped into our world...to give us the greatest miracle of all—eternal life. While He journeyed on this earth, He performed miracles, just to give us a glimpse of His power. Jesus first turned water to wine—providing not a need, but an overflow of life. As He traveled with His disciples, the Bible says He performed MANY miracles. He healed diseases, demanded the demon possessed be freed, and cleansed lepers.

And He didn't stop there. Those miracles were mere child's play in the eyes of the doubtful crowds. Instead, He took the disciples into a raging storm and then caused it to come to a halt by His words alone. As if that were not enough, he healed a paralytic lying on a mat; healed a bleeding woman (not through His will, but *through her faith*); raised a dead girl and a dear friend to life; made a blind man see, a mute man speak; fed five thousand near Bethsaida Julius with just five loaves and two fish (He even performed that miracle again, just because the disciples seemed to forget!); and then thought it would be life changing to walk on water. We'd like to think if WE had been there, we would have believed! How could you not? But by the Gospel writers' own admission, they doubted... *even after all the miracles.*

It was when they came to a crowd near the northeastern shore of the Sea of Galilee that the gathering of people became overwhelming; they had no food, so the disciples began to panic. What? That's right... they were distraught, and as a last resort sought Jesus's help. Again He performed the miracle of feeding four thousand... that was after He had already fed five thousand back in Decapolis! They even had leftovers to bring with them! (God provides beyond all our needs.)

Yet as they continued their travels, they forgot the bread. (We tend to forget all that God has provided us as well.) So they began panicking again and Jesus overheard them. Jesus had a few words for them, and for us:

> "You have so little faith! Why are you arguing with each other about having no bread? Don't you understand even yet? ***Don't you remember*** the 5,000 I fed with the five

loaves, and the baskets of leftovers you picked up? Or the 4,000 I fed with seven loaves, and the large baskets of left-overs you picked up?"
(Matthew 16:8–20 NLT)

We can't imagine what the disciples must have been feeling at this point. If there were a hole, they likely would have crawled into it. But they couldn't have been feeling any worse than John the Baptist when he, too, questioned Jesus's authenticity.

John was expecting miracles from the Messiah. Not too much to ask, you'd think, since John had prepared the way for Jesus to come into the world...even baptizing Him. But John sat rotting in a prison. (We can understand how John's faith might waver in such circumstances...we've been there in various ways.) And when the disciples came to report the miracles Jesus had been doing, John had one thing to say to Jesus:

"Are you the one who is to come, or should we expect someone else?"
(Luke 7:19 NIV)

Don't we feel the same? When we're in a pit, held captive in the prison of our pain, we wonder if God is who He really says He is...because if He were, we'd expect to be set free.

We'd expect our pain and suffering to end.

Jesus's words in reply are humbling, *but less than comforting:*

"Go back to John and tell him what you have seen and heard—the blind see, the lame walk, the lepers are cured, the deaf hear, the dead are raised to life, and the Good News is preached to the poor.

And tell him, 'God blesses those who do not turn away because of me [And blessed is the one who is not offended by me. ESV]'"
(LUKE 7:22 NLT)

It wasn't long after that John was beheaded. God gave John no miracle. Yet if we're aware of God's ways, then we can see, looking back on history, that God had given John the greatest miracle of all—the miracle *within* himself. The miracle of faith that doesn't demand one's own way, *but accepts God's and does not turn away simply because God doesn't do it their way.* I have not ♥♥♥

Jesus had a few more words about miracles:

"Only an evil, adulterous generation would demand a miraculous sign."
(MATTHEW 16:4 NLT)

He sighed deeply and said, "Why does this generation ask for a sign? Truly I tell you, no sign will be given to it."
(MARK 8:12 NIV)

It is painfully obvious... *miracles don't equal faith.* Our faith walk does not progress with giant leaps forward; we don't gain faith through burning bushes or bolts of lightning. (We forget the miracles far too easily... even dramatic ones.)

Our ancestors in Egypt were not impressed by the LORD's miraculous deeds. They soon forgot his many acts of kindness to them. Instead, they rebelled against him at the Red Sea.

(PSALM 106:7 NLT)

When we're suffering in ways that words cannot express, we want God to speak—OUT LOUD! We want Him to grant us a miraculous deliverance, quickly meet our needs, and remove all our pain and suffering. Is that too much to ask? But God's ways, being higher than our own, don't work that way. God doesn't make deals…i.e., in exchange for a miracle, we'll have faith in Him for the rest of our life. (He's smarter than that.)

In our desperation, He shows us that what produces faith is a Christian who endures trials, storms, pain, and suffering with unwavering faith. It's when our heart is in constant pursuit of His, through the wilderness of life, that we emerge stronger in character, stronger in faith, stronger in Christ…*ready for anything.* And He lovingly points the way: "*The road is this way.*"

"Great," we sarcastically reply, "always wanted to be a part of *Man vs. Wild*." (God likes a sense of humor, by the way…He's got one. If you haven't noticed that, maybe you should get to know Him better!)

So what we find is that the road of faith takes us into the wilderness…and sometimes we, like the Israelites, spend forty years there. But even in the wilderness, God provides

our every need for our journey with Him. He promises His provision and shows His faithfulness even through our doubts. The daily bread from heaven, only enough for that day (see Exodus 16:4), reminds us of our desperate need for God. God wants us to desire Him for who He is, not just what He gives...and over history, we've proven that miracles will never cause us to trust. God knows us better than we know ourselves. We've got *short-term spiritual memory.*

> But despite all the miraculous signs Jesus had done, most of the people **still** did not believe in him.
> (JOHN 12:37 NLT)

God's ways include taking us through times when there are no miracles—no signs to solidify our faith. He's teaching us something. He's teaching us to move on in faith...not according to a vision or a voice, but in the midst of the wilderness—where He is all we have. It's there, in the "dry places" of our lives that we learn *He is all we need.* He wants us to be confident that when we cannot hear His voice or see the path ahead, He's leading us somewhere and we can trust Him. He's making a path. He's at work in your life.

> But he knows the way that I take;
> when he has tested me,
> I will come forth as gold.
> (JOB 23:10 NIV)

Though the path God makes is crooked, mysterious, painful, and paved with tears, *He's made it.* The furnace of affliction may be seven times heated—*He lighted it.* Though the furnace of affliction is hot, we can trust the hand that kindles it. Through His promises, the fires will not consume us, ***but refine us.***

> When you pass through the waters,
> I will be with you; and when you pass
> through the rivers, they will not sweep over you.
> When you walk through the fire,
> you will not be burned;
> the flames will not set you ablaze.
> (ISAIAH 43:2 NIV)

It's the Almighty God who is directing our footsteps. It's His hand that is holding us to the fire, so that we might come forth as gold. *But we prayed for silver.*

> "We pray for silver, but God gives us gold instead."
> —MARTIN LUTHER

Sure, God can part Red Seas, drop bread out of heaven, bring water from a rock, heal, and just for a good shock, walk on water, *but He'd rather do something more miraculous than that*—He'd rather you love Him. He'd rather you know Him.

He'd rather give you what you need, instead of what you want. He wants you to have unshakable faith and trust in

CHERIE HILL

Him. *It's the faith that can't be shaken that's the faith that **has been** shaken.*

A Red Sea Place

Annie Johnson Flint

*Have you come to the Red Sea place in your life
Where in spite of all you can do,
There is no way out.
There is no way back.
There is no other way but through.
Then wait on the Lord with a trust serene
'Til the night of your fear is gone;
He will send the winds,
He will heap the floods,
When He says to your soul, "Go on."
And His hand will lead you through—
clear through
Ere the watery walls roll down,
No foe can reach you,
No wave can touch,
No mightiest sea can drown.
The tossing billows may rear their crests,
Their foam at your feet may break;
But over their bed you shall walk dry shod
In the path that your Lord will make.
In the morning watch, 'neath the lifted cloud,
You shall see but the Lord alone,
When He leads you on from the place of the sea
To a land that you have not known;*

And your fears shall pass as your foes have passed,
You shall be no more afraid;
You shall sing His praise in a better place,
A place that His hand has made.

Although you're overwhelmed and don't have the strength to take one more step, God's laying out the path that He's taking you down . . . you won't be able to travel it in your own strength—*He'll be your guide and your strength.* He's about to show you some things that are beyond miraculous and will forever place your faith on a firm foundation. But before excitement gets the best of you, you probably need to know . . . **this path is a pathway of *brokenness*.**

When my spirit
was overwhelmed within me,
You knew my path.
(Psalm 142:3 NASB)

The pathway of brokenness, the valleys that we find ourselves in throughout life, are simply *the avenue whereby God's heart transforms ours.*

"But then I will win her back once again.
I will lead her into the desert
and speak tenderly to her there.
I will return her vineyards to her and
transform the Valley of Trouble
into a gateway of hope."
(Hosea 2:14–15 NLT)

The Pathway to Brokenness

Sometimes we get on this path by our own wrongdoings; more often, we had nothing to do with it at all. Author Philip Yancey, in his priceless book *Where Is God When It Hurts?*, gives ample explanation for the cause of suffering in this world:

> "Much of the suffering on our planet has come about because of two principles that God built into creation: a physical world that runs according to consistent natural laws, and human freedom."

No matter the cause, God is with us. And no matter how difficult the trial, we're told to consider it all joy.

Dear brothers and sisters,
when troubles come your way,
consider it be an opportunity for great joy.
(JAMES 1:2 NLT)

As if our trials in life were not difficult enough, God allows a statement like *that* to be printed . . . adding an even greater burden to the ones we're already crumbling beneath. But God knows what He's talking about. These times of trials, this pathway of brokenness, is part of a process. It's His *work in progress*.

Just as we crush grapes to make wine and grind wheat for bread . . . God is breaking us so that He might transform our lives completely. God works through our weaknesses, insults, distresses, persecutions, and difficulties, for Christ's sake and for our own. It's when *you are weak* ... He is strong:

 For when I am weak, then I am strong.
(2 CORINTHIANS 12:10 NIV)

Why are we strong when we are weak? It's because we are no longer relying on ourselves to save us ... *we're relying on the only One who can—God.*

God didn't choose just anyone to write these words. He chose Paul, one who had murdered those who had worshipped Christ, had been converted on the road to Damascus, and then, after sacrificing his life for the gospel, wound up beaten, imprisoned, and shipwrecked. *That's* when he wrote these words. Not in the midst of great miracles, or in mountaintop moments. Paul found God, more times than not, in brokenness. *And so will we.*

In 2 Corinthians 4:17 (NIV), Paul learned something that we tend to forget:

 Our present sufferings are a brief,
but important part of a larger plan ...
one day, it will all be worthwhile.

Paul trusted in God's greater good and so must we. Yet although this may make perfectly good sense to an all-knowing God, *it simply makes no sense at all to us.* We are haunted by the truth that *"His ways are higher."* If we can come to view our lives in light of God's long-term

glory instead of our short-term happiness, we take one step further into being transformed into the likeness of Christ... which is exactly what God is doing. He's working on us, out of love,

to make us more like Jesus.

And I am certain that God, who began a good work within you, will continue his work until it is finally finished on the day when Christ Jesus returns.
(PHILIPPIANS 1:6 NLT)

If we won't humble ourselves before God, He'll do it for us. He loves us that much. What we learn upon our knees is that this life is not about us. It's foremost about the purposes, plan, and glory of God.

We don't need to run from suffering or lose hope if God doesn't remove it... we must trust that *God has a perfectly good purpose for allowing all that He permits.* But it's just not that easy, is it?

We, like Jesus, feel that maybe, just maybe, there's another way. Quite possibly this pathway through brokenness isn't all that necessary. But God seems to think He knows best. And if we'll stop for a moment, we should consider how many times (probably never) we have ever heard someone say, "*I grew closest to God when my life was free of pain and suffering.*"

Though we question God's ways, He never changes (see Malachi 3:6), so we might as well settle in for the journey. At times He may take us around this path; more often than not, *He won't*. But He takes our hand, protects and provides, and carries us when we're too weak to travel on.

God may, at times, deliver us from suffering, but more often than not, He sustains us. Though the pathway of brokenness doesn't appear to show any resemblance of mercy or grace, suffering leads us to repentance and humility—bringing us to a place of trusting God. It's God's grace... *disguised.* As our heart is breaking, *God is beckoning us to receive the fullness of His.*

Our brokenness is God's way of dealing with our pride—the desire within us to act independently from Him. No matter how matured we are in our faith, we continually fight the temptation to do things our way, rather than His.

If we choose our way, instead of God's, we hinder our relationship with Him and delay the fulfillment of His will in our lives—we remain in the wilderness... with the potential of dying there.

We deceive ourselves. We should be thankful for pain, which alerts us to our true condition. It's pain that gives us the ability to know pleasure. Pain is not meant to work against you. We shouldn't try to avoid pain and suffering, but understand its purpose: to turn us to God, to demand that we come to terms with our need for help... divine help... *our need for God.* And that... *is the purpose for our pain.*

*But this happened that we might not rely on
ourselves, but on God who raises the dead.*

(2 CORINTHIANS 1:9 NIV)

*Show me my purpose Father ...? To just be Still, and
me my purpose a son ...C 12:33 6.12.16 CAD.
know him as Son*

The Purpose of Pain

To believe that there is purpose in pain is simply difficult, at best, to grasp. But there ARE purposes for it. This pathway of brokenness, this work that God is doing in us, through it, may seem like a high price to pay for faith...but that's because *we tend to underestimate faith's value.*

> *"Our pain and suffering is never wasted. God uses it all.
> It's when we suffer that our heart is more accessible to the
> voice of God."*
> —CHERIE HILL

Pain is a tool in the hand of God. He uses our sufferings to bring us to the end of ourselves and back into His arms. Isn't that worth any cost? Maybe so, but it will take our faith awhile to agree...that's why God is taking us down this path...He has things to teach us and show us along the way.

Our faith is a journey, not a destination. The furnace may be a painful process, but the reality is, as some Chinese Christians say: *True gold does not fear the fire.*

Though we walk through a valley, *a shadow of death,* when we get to the other side of it, when we've gone through it, God knows we'll have an absolute confidence in Him. We'll have the assurance that God will walk with

Then the revelation the Holy Spirit Shared me... I'm, if you don't treasure me during this "wooing stage" how will I treasure me once you've got me? And T. H.S. said - if you don't have a relationship w/ me now, you will when all is happy and...

us throughout the remainder of our lives. We'll experi- *peacful* ence His faithfulness and be less inclined to fear...*for* *Oh* *He is with us.* The valley produces the kind of Christlike *my.* perseverance that will lead us home. God never wastes our *I un-* suffering...*there are purposes for our pain.* *derstand...*

Paul reveals just a few of God's purposes through our pain. He reveals God's ways to us in order that we might have joy. You see, there's more to James 1:2. Paul goes on to show us that through our pain, God is at work...doing *good* things.

James 1:3–4 (NLT) reveals God's ways for every valley in life:

> For you know that when your faith is tested,
> your endurance has a chance to grow.
> So let it grow, for when your endurance is fully developed,
> you will be perfect and complete,
> needing nothing.

God wants us ready for *anything.* We need to be ready for anything and everything in this life. No one has to tell you that.

> "A faith that leaves us unprepared for suffering   *That's*
> is a false faith that deserves to be lost.   *what I*
> Suffering will come; we owe it to God, ourselves,   *had -*
> and those around us to prepare for it."
> —RANDY ALCORN, *If God Is Good*

For faith to be genuine, *it must be tested.* There's no way for this "cup to pass." In order for anything to be strength-

ened, it must meet resistance. It's easy to trust God when all is well, but can you sing "All is Well with My Soul" when you're financially ruined, when you're back to work at an age when your body is falling apart, when your spouse walks out unexpectedly, when your child's disease takes a turn for the worse, when doubt is pounding down your door and you have no strength to keep it out? When times get tough, our faith can take a nosedive. In moments like these, it appears we're flunking the test. We're hoping God grades on the curve. But instead, He reaches down, takes us by the hand, and *embraces us with His grace.*

In desperate situations of life, our faith has a collision between high hopes and harsh realities. In the depths of our darkness we grasp this truth:

> *"Until all you have is faith, you don't know it's all you need."*
> —CHERIE HILL

So, this test of faith has qualities of its own. For starters, Paul says it produces endurance. It's not necessarily what we'd desire—we're hoping this journey of faith is a sprint, *not a marathon.* When suffering is draining the life out of us, we're convinced that endurance is not something we're interested in achieving. Yet even in our resistance, God sovereignly and lovingly protects us by determining the length and intensity of every trial (see the Biblical book of Job).

Although we may not think we can endure, God knows our limits and won't go beyond them. If we can trust God in that way, *we can find the strength to take just one more step.* God's goal for us in our pain and suffering is that we patiently abide in the trial with an attitude of unfailing trust in His *goodness.*

God wants to bring us to a place in our faith where we have a firm determination to live for His purposes, regardless of the cost.

> *"On the other hand, would you know who is the greatest Saint in the world: It is not he who prays most or fasts most; it is not he who gives most alms, or is most eminent for temperance, chastity, or justice; but he who is always thankful to God, who wills everything that God willeth, who receives everything as an instance of God's goodness, and has a heart always ready to praise God for it."*
> —WILLIAM LAW, *A Serious Call to a Devout and Holy Life*

But it's not all about endurance. God's long-term vision for us is that we would be "fully developed," or as some translations put it, "perfect and complete." Surrendering to God, making Him Lord of your life, goes far beyond baptism and a one-time confession of faith—it's just the beginning. God's desire is that we would become mature in our faith...conforming to the image of His Son.

It's in our trials, our sufferings, our moments of crying, *"Why, God, Why?"* that we are closer to Christ than we have ever been. Our faith, learning to trust God, is a lifelong process. He uses the fire to bring impurities to the surface, so that we might seek His help in overcoming every hindrance that holds us back from His best in our lives.

Therefore, since we are surrounded by such a huge crowd of witnesses to the life of faith, let us strip off every weight that slows us down, especially the sin that so easily trips us up. And let us run with endurance the race God has set before us.
(HEBREWS 12:1 NLT)

Until we reflect Christ in every area of our lives, we are a *work in progress*. As the reality of God's ways and this path He is paving sets in, we realize we may be in this valley *a little longer than we had hoped*.

If we're to be ready for anything, or lacking in nothing, by our own admission we'd say God has a lot of work to do in us. The most surprising of all the purposes in our pain is that we might develop the right *attitude* through each and every trial. Evidently, God thinks that through our suffering we need an attitude adjustment. He's probably right. We're not exactly content when our home is foreclosed upon. We're not exactly finding it all joy when cancer is the diagnosis. In fact, anger and resentment seem more fitting in circumstances like these. But God is at work in us and as He's teaching us to trust Him, He's also showing us that we need to do it with the right attitude. *Help me Father.*

So, to keep me from becoming proud, I was given my thorn in my flesh, a messenger from Satan to torment me and keep me from becoming proud. Three different times I begged the Lord to take it away. Each time he said, "My grace is all you need. My power works best in weakness."

So now I am glad to boast about my weaknesses, so that the power of Christ can work through me. That's why I take pleasure in my weaknesses, and in the insults, hardships, persecutions, and troubles that I suffer for Christ.
(2 CORINTHIANS 12:7–10 NLT)

Whatever our "thorn in the flesh" is...we're to take pleasure *in* it. Knowing our thoughts about this thorn, we're thinking God bit off a little more than He could chew when it comes to working on this part of our faith. He's asking us to do the impossible! Once again we get it wrong...*He's not asking us to do anything*...He's only asking us to rely on His grace...which makes ALL things possible.

In the wise words of Philip Yancey (*Where Is God When It Hurts?*), "[pain] and *suffering can serve as instruments to teach us the value of dependence, and unless we learn dependence we will never experience grace.*"

As Philip Yancey investigates the purposes for our pain and suffering, he stumbles across "advantages" of pain and suffering—quite a discovery in many ways. No one ever thinks of pain and suffering as being advantageous. But one nun, Monika Hellwig, whom Yancey references, lists those advantages and Yancey expands upon them:

1. *Suffering, the great equalizer, brings us to a point where we may realize our urgent need for redemption.*
2. *Those who suffer know not only their dependence on God and on healthy people but also the interdependence with one another.*

3. Those who suffer rest their security not in one thing, which often cannot be enjoyed and may soon be taken away, but rather on people.

4. Those who suffer have no exaggerated sense of their own importance, and no exaggerated need of privacy. Suffering humbles the proud.

5. Those who suffer expect little from competition and much from cooperation.

6. Suffering helps us distinguish between necessities and luxuries.

7. Suffering teaches patience, often a kind of dogged patience born of acknowledged dependence.

8. Suffering teaches the difference between valid fears and exaggerated fears.

9. To suffering people, the gospel sounds like good news and not like a threat or a scolding. It offers hope and comfort.

10. Those who suffer can respond to the call of the gospel with a certain abandonment and uncomplicated totality because they have so little to lose and are ready for anything.

Yancey goes on to list the great qualities of a "prized" spiritual life: dependence, humility, simplicity, cooperation, being abandoned to God. And that is how God uses pain and suffering. He brings us to a place of trusting Him...of relying on Him completely. In this world, there is *no greater advantage*.

If we'll trust Him, He'll grow our faith in ways that we can never imagine (see Ephesians 3:20). Truly, nothing is too difficult for God! ✓

For **nothing**
is impossible with God.
(LUKE 1:37 NLT)

In the face of impossibilities, God is at work within us through our pain and suffering, and what He accomplishes in the process is *far more precious* than gold (see 1 Peter 1:7).

> "God uses suffering to purge sin from our lives, strengthen our commitment to him, force us to depend on his grace, bind us together with other believers, produce discernment, foster sensitivity, discipline our minds, impart wisdom, stretch our hope, cause us to know Christ better, make us long for truth, lead us to repentance of sin, teach us to give thanks in times of sorrow, increase our faith, and strengthen our character."
> —RANDY ALCORN, *If God Is Good*

God's purposes go far beyond anything we could hope for or imagine (see Ephesians 3:20). His desire is that we would know Him in an intimate way. He wants our faith to go beyond simply summoning miraculous signs and wonders. He wants us to learn to truly trust Him, *even in His silence.* He wants to give us an extraordinary measure of faith that will carry us through this life, so that we might live without fear, until we see Him face-to-face. He wants

us to draw near to Him so that He might draw near to us. He wants us to walk with Him awhile... *through the valley of adversity.*

Walking with God

From David to Paul, the message of God is clear: God wants us lacking *nothing*. Even Adam and Eve had everything in the garden in abundance. But now we must choose the way *we'll* walk—the abundance God gave us in the beginning just didn't seem to be enough. And although we'd like to think we would have handled things in the garden differently, *we wouldn't have*.

We know Adam and Eve walked with God in the garden because they hid from Him one day. We tend to hide *every* day. Our agenda seems to push God's aside and, quite frankly, at times He just cramps our style. We're convinced that His way is not the best way and He should just stick to taking care of His matters in heaven, since He can't seem to get it right down here. In a moment of insanity, we prepare our résumé and await God to show us His. Guess who's better qualified? *Right answer.*

Even through our pride and arrogance, God still loves us. And although we'd like to think that the life of faith is about trusting in a God who gives us things, we encounter a rude awakening when we realize that what He really wants to give us is Himself...which is *everything*. Our valleys of life are an invitation to walk with God...to get to know Him personally. He's inviting you to a life of faith that goes far beyond knowing about Him.

> "The life of faith is not about things we understand;
> it is about things we believe.
> It is less about the things
> we can know about God
> and more about the things
> that draw us to God."
> —ROBERT BENSON, *In Constant Prayer*

You may know right from wrong in many areas of your life, but do you know *why* God wants you to live a certain way? Do you know *what* motivates Him? Do you know *how* He acts and *why* He acts in that way? In the valley of adversity, we come to a place where our hunger and thirst to know God becomes more than just a mere pleasure, but a *desperate need*.

> As the deer pants for streams of water,
> so my soul pants for you, my God.
> My soul thirsts for God,
> for the living God.
> (PSALM 42:1–2 NIV)

This walk with God is so that we might learn about Him, in order that He might transform our faith. You see, God could have spared you from the pain and suffering in

your life, but it was not His will, His way, or His plan for your life. He has greater things He wants to teach you, and they can only be learned through sorrow and suffering.

God uses our suffering to redeem and to restore. It is His grace, which is sufficient in all things, that moves His heart to show you His ways through His word, so that you might know and experience the great depths of His love for you. If you're walking with God, you have the greatest source of knowledge, love, peace, joy, and hope abiding *within* you. Nothing is more valuable...*not even gold.* And especially not the "thing" you're asking Him for in life. If you'll trust Him, one day He'll make you another divine exchange: your *cross* will get you a *crown*...and you'll have the joy of casting it at the feet of Jesus (see Revelation 4:10).

> *Blessed is the one who perseveres under trial because, having stood the test, that person will receive the crown of life that the Lord has promised to those who love him.*
> (JAMES 1:12 NIV)

It's hard to comprehend that the God of the universe wants to have a personal, intimate relationship with us, but since the beginning of time He's been wooing us. Through the Bible, He has written His love letters to us, in order to draw us near to Him.

> *Come near to God and He will come near to you.*
> (JAMES 4:8 NIV)

We can't understand and walk in God's will if we do not learn His ways. He reveals His ways through His word and through personal revelations, when we go to Him *continually* in prayer. The saints of the Bible learned the ways of God through trials and difficulties, *and so must we.* Pain does not serve its full purpose if we are merely alerted when it is present. Pain must hurt, so that it causes change.

God is bringing our faith to a place where we don't desire Him only for what He gives, but for who He is. He sees the depths of our hearts, our selfish desires, and He'll leave us in the furnace until our hearts are ready to be made His. He's waiting to hear our hearts pierce His with:

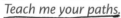

> *Make me to know Your ways, O LORD;*
> *Teach me your paths.*
> *Lead me in Your truth and teach me...*
> (PSALM 25:4–5 NASB)

As we seek Him with humble hearts through prayer, we will find that He is truly sovereign, His ways are perfect, and His plans are *always* best. We may not understand why He moves things in a certain direction, but He will give us assurance that His heart is full of love for us through all the uncertainty.

Allowing God to lead and guide us through His truth enables us to face life without fear. But in order to know God, we need to have a desire, commitment, and love for Him. The more we give of ourselves to Him, the more He

gives of Himself to us. The more we trust Him, the more He will do for us.

> *Oh, that my people would listen to me,*
> *that Israel would walk in my ways!*
> *I would soon subdue their enemies*
> *and turn my hand against their foes.*
> (PSALM 81:13–14 ESV)

Through this word from Him, we hear His heart crying out to Israel, *and to us*. He's calling us to expand our faith...to take just one more step with Him. He's asking us to trust Him. If you will, He'll show you that He'll do MORE than you can imagine in your life (see Ephesians 3:20). He longs for us to walk in His ways. If we could just get a glimpse of all that He has planned for us, we'd see the very best is ahead.

> *So be truly glad. There is wonderful joy ahead, even though*
> *you have to endure many trials for a little while.*
> (1 PETER 1:6 NLT)

God knows what is best for us. Only He knows what the future holds. Many times we're standing at the doorway of blessings, but we want our way, our desires, and our rights, and we go through the wrong door. We take the wrong path...and when this happens, *we end up missing God's very best.*

We reason within ourselves and declare, "When I can understand God and see Him, *then I'll trust Him.*" But that's not the way it works—*believing is seeing.*

> Then Jesus told him, "You believe because you have seen me. **Blessed *are those who believe without seeing me.*"**
> (JOHN 20:29 NLT)

We can find ourselves drawing near to God, only to discover that the faith required to be in relationship with Him is wavering. Sometimes God *doesn't* move mountains; sometimes doubt creeps in because we trusted Him and His promises, but too much time has gone by—*nothing's changed.*

In the words of Philip Yancey, "our cry of 'Where is God when it hurts?'" becomes a plea of deeper desperation... "*Where is God when it* won't stop *hurting?*" Through our tears, we must be determined not to allow our feelings to govern how we view God's ways and His goodness.

We must refuse to allow anything to come between ourselves and God. We must always put our faith between us and our circumstances. Our faith must be unfaltering and our spirit steadfast. We must *always* view our lives through God's promises to us. And if you're waiting patiently for a promise God has made to you to unfold, don't give up... *He may be just about ready to roll your stone away.*

We must know God in order to trust Him. We must be dedicated in getting to know Him so that we are prepared

for the trials of life before they ever occur. We can't forget that it *wasn't* raining when Noah built the ark. He trusted God's word to Him. *Though nothing was happening,* he continued to obey God even when nothing in the physical world said that he should. He never asked God "Why?" *He just had faith.* He didn't demand that God give him the exact date in which the flood would come. He didn't argue with God over His ways, he just did what he was told.

Day in and day out, Noah sought God. And most of all, *Noah didn't become discouraged.* Noah was watchful, trusting, and patient as he waited for God's plan to unfold. He had great faith because *he walked with God.* Because he walked with Him, he trusted Him, and he left all the details to the One who controlled them. If we want great faith, the faith that moves mountains . . . we must walk with God too.

As we draw near to Him and begin walking with Him in our daily lives, we find that He rarely shows us anything more about our journey than just the very next step ahead of us. If He showed us the entire map, we might get tempted to go ahead of Him. He wants to lead us, *step-by-step,* so that He can make a path to fulfill His plan. Only He has the supernatural power to change men's hearts, take down giants in the land, and provide for our every need along the journey. We can't anticipate what lies ahead, but we can trust that God knows.

It's your trust in Him that will build a bridge of faith that will take you from this world to the next.

When you walk, your steps will not be hampered;
when you run, you will not stumble.
(PROVERBS 4:12 NIV)

Long ago, there was such a thing as a self-opening gate, which was used on country roads. It stood firm across the road as travelers approached it. If you stopped before you got to it...it wouldn't open. But if you drove right at it, the wagon wheels would press the springs below the roadway and the gate would swing back to let you through. *We too must press through.* We must trust in God to go ahead of us in our journey. We must trust that He knows the way we take. We must not pay attention to the obstacle. If we come to a river, *God will dry it up.* If it's a mountain, *God can move it. And if He doesn't, we can trust He's got a better way.*

God may never give us all the details behind His plans and purposes for our lives. In fact, *don't count on it.* But if you'll seek Him, walk with Him, and obey Him, He will reveal everything you need for the very next step ahead of you. We can't always know His will, *but we can pray it.* God is working, regardless of what we see. There are NO limits to what God can do. We must never calculate a situation without adding in the faithfulness of God. We can trust, through God's promises, that He alone sets the perimeters of our trials and will not allow us to be tried beyond the ability that He gives us to endure.

Rest assured God knows your doubts and fears. He understands why, at times, we stumble in our faith and let doubt get the best of us.

He knows the reasons we hesitate to obey...but none of this changes God's mind or His ways. He conveys to you through His word that His love for you is infinite, unconditional, and long-suffering. When you face pain and suffering, *He faces it with you.* When you must walk through a valley that seems to never end, *He goes before you to shine light in the darkness.* Don't try and figure God out. Don't seek to limit God. And don't assume what God will and will not do. These are potholes in your faith walk.

The benefits of walking with God *far outweigh* the risks. You're walking with the One who is all knowing—nothing happens outside of God's knowledge and He is able to do the impossible. If you're walking with God, you couldn't be advised by anyone with more wisdom—He is all wise. And mostly, God's love is infinite. His love is not limited in any way. The valley of the shadow of death is just a *shadow.*

And He's with you. If you'll trust Him, allowing Him to lead you step-by-step...He's taking you somewhere. There are green pastures up ahead for you to lie down and rest. There are quiet waters to sit by as He refreshes your soul. And along the way...God comforts you. *He's guiding you along the right paths*...and yes, it's right through the valley (see Psalm 23:3).

You may not know where you're going, *but God does.* You can't always know His will, *but you can trust it.*

3

Hope Being Gone

What we wanted didn't happen. What did happen isn't what we wanted, and *hopelessness* is the result. Our faith has gotten us this far, but it appears to be the end of the road. *All hope seems gone.* Though we trusted God was with us, we're now feeling utterly and completely *alone.* Even though we believe, *we doubt*...and although we may, in fact, believe that God knows what He's doing, *we're not on board with His plan.*

We've traveled with Him a fair amount of time now in this valley, and *we're not seeing green pastures.* The quiet waters that once brought us peace now rage to flood stage—*fear has set in.* We've taken steps of faith, but it's hard to believe that God is really in control...*because life sure isn't.*

It appears completely obvious that *we're* not in control. Helplessness has consumed us to the point that we're paralyzed. Yet although we've realized that we're not in control,

we're not exactly convinced that God is either. We look around to ask God some pointed questions, yet He's nowhere to be found. Maybe He's forgotten His promises. Maybe He's just not aware of what's going on. There has to be *some* explanation for His lack of intervention. We've waited in faith, but nothing's changed. Nothing's gotten better. And our "*not yet*" seems to have become a "*not ever.*" There no longer appears to be a reason for hope.

> *Even when there was no reason for hope,*
> *Abraham kept hoping…*
> *And Abraham's faith did not weaken…*
> *Abraham never wavered in believing God's promise.*
> *In fact, his faith grew stronger, and in this he brought glory*
> *to God. He was fully convinced that God*
> *is able to do whatever he promises.*
> (ROMANS 4:18–21 NLT)

When the storms of life become catastrophic and the winds of adversity keep us from standing, we're looking for anything and everything to hold on to. To keep our vessel from being lost at sea, we could use our anchor—hope. But that anchor, too, is drifting; in fact it even seems to be *pulling us into* hopelessness.

> *We have this hope as an anchor*
> *for the soul, firm and secure.*
> (HEBREWS 6:19 NIV)

It's Hopeless

We've trusted that God works all things for good, yet things have gotten worse. We were walking with Him, but He's suddenly *walked off*. Hopelessness sets in as a result. But God is *always* at work. He uses ALL things... *even hopelessness.*

We can rest assured that this hopeless place is just a stop along our journey. God's using it to get our full attention. (We begrudgingly agree that He's got it!)

The truth is that hopeless situations are allowed by God. Hopelessness helps us to realize that we need God's help.

The pages of the Bible are filled with events that are *completely* hopeless. We can look at Noah, Moses, David, and even Jesus. (Not to mention the hopeless situations of all those whom Jesus healed.) Our hopelessness is part of our journey, *not our final destination.* Hopelessness opens our eyes that we should pursue God to a greater degree. Anything that draws us near to God is good for us. And often, our hopeless condition is where we tend to experience God the most.

> ... *strengthening the disciples and encouraging them to remain true to the faith.*
> *"We must go through many hardships to enter the kingdom of God," they said.*
> (ACTS 14:22 NIV)

73

Like it or not, hopeless situations are the true test of our faith. The questions that beg answers are: "*Will we stand firm in our faith and cling to what God has promised in His word? Or will we allow our circumstances to dictate our faith in Him?*" And listen, it's not that God needs to know the answers... *He wants you to know them.* He's using hopelessness to bring things to the surface. You may have been confident in your faith, but God saw something that needed working on.

> *If you think you are standing strong,*
> *be careful not to fall.*
> (1 CORINTHIANS 10:12 NLT)

We try desperately to create our own hope. We look for things to hope *in* and hope *for*... we lose track of the One from whom hope comes. Hope is the result of clinging to God *despite* the seeming hopelessness of our situation.

> *Though he slay me, **yet** will I hope in him.*
> (JOB 13:15 NIV)

Hopelessness has a way of stripping life down to the essentials. We tend to grasp what really matters in life when we're hopeless. Seems God really *does* know what He's doing. (We just wish there were another way.) These times of helplessness show us that we have our hope in the wrong places. In our darkest days and hardest nights, we come to understand our need for TRUE hope. Without hope in God, life loses its meaning and our heart gets sick.

Hope deferred makes the heart sick.
(PROVERBS 13:12 NIV)

It's our heart's sickness that causes us to realize we need the Great Physician to heal us. Jesus said, *"It's not the healthy who need a doctor, but the sick"* (Mark 2:17 NIV).

Jesus came to bind up our broken hearts (see Isaiah 61:1) and give us hope. But we need to realize that we're sick. We have to *want* to be healed.

Through our desperate need for healing and hope, we come to grips with the fact that there are things *we can't* control, things that are *not for us* to control, and we're reminded that God is God and we are not. (Thank God for that!)

When we're struggling to *survive*, God has found a place where He can *thrive*. Sometimes He allows us to experience extreme weakness and despair just so we can experience His supernatural strength. As we're struggling to understand the ways of God, He reminds us that sometimes there is no other explanation for our pain and suffering, but just so that He might bring glory to Himself and strengthen our faith and the faith of others. Sometimes we're broken just so God can heal us. Such was the case with the blind man—*it might be the case with you.*

As Jesus and His disciples traveled, they came across a man who was blind. His disciples thought it a good opportunity to try to understand the ways of God and asked Jesus, "Rabbi, who sinned, this man or his parents, that he was born blind?"

75

His reply was not what they were expecting. They got more than they bargained for—*a miracle*. Jesus said, *"Neither this man nor his parents sinned, but this happened so that the works of God might be displayed in him"* (see John 9:1–12, NIV). Sometimes things happen for reasons that can only be known to God.

Often we must live with circumstances that bring no understanding for years, even decades, and *possibly never* on this side of eternity. Though it is impossible to understand the dynamic ways of God, *we can trust in the One who heals us*. He has reasons for all He *does* and all He *allows*. Besides, He knows that knowing the answer as to exactly why He permits specific sufferings wouldn't change anything anyway—truly, would knowing the *reasons* take away even one ounce of the pain you're enduring? *He didn't think so.*

God can do anything, but what He really wants to do is make your heart His. He wants to heal your brokenness in a way that changes your life forever. He wants to transform your tragedy into triumph and give you beauty for your ashes (see Isaiah 61:3). And like it or not, He'll stop at nothing to do His job. If He doesn't change your situation... *He'll change you!* And He's famously known for doing *both*.

Despite the apparent hopelessness in our lives, real hope comes from faith in God. God is committed to working within His children through every circumstance. He is less concerned about our comfort and more interested in developing our character. If changing our circumstances will hinder our character development, we can be sure that God is in no hurry to change them. Hope will be born out of our trust in God, as He works within us. If we'll allow Him to, He will transform our lives through making us humble, teach us to surrender every circumstance to His care and accept the situations He has allowed in our lives, and enable us to walk obediently into the blessings He has in store for us:

> "What no eye has seen, what no ear has heard,
> and what no human mind has conceived
> the things God has prepared for those who love him."
>
> (1 CORINTHIANS 2:9 NIV)

Things may seem hopeless, but absolutely nothing is truly hopeless when you're trusting God. Trust His hand and trust His watch. Grab hold of His promises and don't let go!

> You have a ticket to heaven no thief can take,
> an eternal home no divorce can break.
> Every sin of your life has been cast to the sea.
> Every mistake you've made is nailed to the tree.
> You're blood-bought and heaven-made.
> A child of God—forever saved.
> So be grateful, joyful—for isn't it true?
> What you don't have is much less than what you do.
>
> —MAX LUCADO, *A Love Worth Giving*

Though we're told by God that He is everything we need, *we're just not exactly sure we believe that.* If we did have all we need, why do we have moments of darkness that sweep over us in the midst of our faith?

> *Why am I discouraged? Why is my heart so sad? I will put my hope in God! I will praise Him again—my Savior and my God! Now I am deeply discouraged, but I will remember you...*
> (PSALM 42:5–6 NLT)

Hopelessness in the hands of God is a means by which God alerts our hearts that our faith will not stand the test of time, nor the trials of life, if we are not intimate with Him, trusting in Him fully, and constantly *fleeing into His presence.*

Why Pray?

In our hopelessness, we desperately need to hear from God. We're certain that He's left us, yet His word says He never leaves us or forsakes us, so if He's not there, we have to ask ourselves, *"Who moved?"* We wonder where God's gone, but fail to recognize that He's right where we left Him. Quite possibly it wasn't God who walked away from our daily walk... *maybe we did.*

God knows we'll lose sight of Him as we journey this life; there are *many* distractions, but He's given us a special privilege as His children... *He's given us prayer.* And prayer is powerful. It allows us to cast our burdens on God and receive His grace, guidance, and provision. With such ready access to Almighty God, *it's a wonder why we ever try to do anything in life without Him.*

If we're willing to surrender our will to His and seek Him earnestly, *He will respond.* We might not get the answer we wanted, but we can be assured that it's for our best.

We either trust Him or we don't. We either believe He is for us or He's not; if we're not sure, we should ask Him... *through prayer.*

When we pray, we are recognizing that God is Sovereign over the universe; we're acknowledging that God is in absolute control of all things.

> The LORD has made the heavens his throne;
> from there he rules over everything.
> (PSALM 103:19 NLT)

Prayer moves the heart and hand of God when we acknowledge Him as Almighty God. But He's not just a *loving* God... He's a *holy* God. His holiness demands justice and it is prayer that helps us to recognize that we fall short of God's absolute holiness. We quickly come to realize that we should approach Him with reverence and awe. Through prayer, we're looking to God instead of ourselves... we're declaring Him Lord of our life, *not just Savior.*

Though we'd love to just bust through the gates of heaven and approach God's throne of grace on our own, we're not allowed to. God has deemed Jesus as the go-to person. And if we must come to Jesus, then we must face our sin. So each and every time we come before God in prayer, He only hears us when we've confessed our sin and asked for forgiveness. We can pray:

> Search me, God, and know my heart;
> test me and know my anxious thoughts.
> See if there is any offensive way in me,
> and lead me in the way everlasting.
>
> (PSALM 139:23–24 NIV)

You see, this journey is going to be a long one in many aspects—incredibly short in others. We can't possibly go the distance with excess baggage. We need to QUICKLY rid ourselves of the sin that causes us to struggle through the journey. Purity of heart and the power of God are connected . . . *prayer makes them possible.*

If we'll confess and repent and forgive others, God promises to hear us. And it's our unceasing prayer that brings about deliverance.

> And will not God bring about justice for his
> chosen ones, who cry out to him day and night?
> Will he keep putting them off? I tell you,
> he will see that they get justice, and quickly.
>
> (LUKE 18:7–8 NIV)

Yet as we pray, instead of praying about the things that break our hearts, we need to focus upon the things that break His. Too often when we pray, we've failed to pray as we've been instructed to—"*Thy Kingdom come, thy will be done.*"

Our privilege of prayer becomes our greatest failure. People all over the world recite the Lord's Prayer daily, and yet have no intention of anyone's will being done *but their own*. We're praying not that God's will be done, *but that He approves ours*.

We must be committed to constant prayer while rejoicing in hope by trusting in His promises.

> *Be joyful in hope, patient in affliction,*
> *faithful in prayer.*
> (Romans 12:12 NIV)

It is through prayer that we invite God into our world, so that He might lead, guide, and direct us each and every moment of our lives. Our privilege in prayer is not that He will hear us, *but that we will hear Him*.

Through prayer we may receive the answer we were hoping for, and *we may not*. It's all about God's will. And if we trust Him, then we can accept His answer . . . no matter what that is. And if we can't . . . *then we don't have a prayer problem, we have a faith problem*. We may need to go back to the basics . . . *the reason for our hope*.

We may need to spend more time with God. It may take forty-two chapters of our lives, as it did with Job. But as Job learned, it was necessary to take his case to God. And

in the end, just like Job, we find that it's our response to the trials of our lives, when all the props of faith are removed, that will either prove our faith or disprove it. And don't despair, life gets tough, we make mistakes, and our faith falters...even God's most loyal believers have moments of hopelessness and despair that overtake them.

> *"Even today my complaint is bitter;*
> *his hand is heavy in spite of my groaning."*
> (JOB 23:2 NIV)

Don't worry, God is ready to listen. And at the right time, *He'll speak.* He's interested in what you have to say to Him. He won't interrupt you...He'll wait until you're finished pouring out your heart. But when He speaks, you'll realize the privilege of prayer is, in itself, its own miracle. Truly, what you'll find is that *you have everything you need.* You can have hope because God is hope himself.

> *You have a God who hears you,*
> *the power of love behind you,*
> *the Holy Spirit within you,*
> *and all of heaven ahead of you.*
> *If you have the Shepherd,*
> *you have grace for every sin,*
> *direction for every turn,*
> *a candle for every corner,*
> *and an anchor for every storm.*
> *You have everything you need.*
> —MAX LUCADO, *Traveling Light*

Hoping in Faith

When difficulties come, when the trials of life invite themselves into our lives unwelcomed (they will: see John 16:33), we can usually get through a few days, even maybe a few months, but as the trial lingers, our faith begins to fail and hope starts to fade. Our problems appear to be even too big for God.

We're told to remember Abraham, who, *"all hope being gone, hoped in faith."* There is always hope in Christ. When all hope seems gone, *there's the cross*...and it points us to where we need to be looking—up.

In our hopelessness, we must set aside feelings and get back to the facts of our faith. We must draw near to God over and over again...and He will restore our hope. Through our prayers God helps us to see our problems from His perspective.

He may be using your situation of suffering to prepare you to be a comfort to others (see 2 Corinthians 1:4). It's about His will, His glory, and His purposes for good.

"Augustine's *Confessions* contains a remarkably similar passage. 'What is it, therefore,' he begins, 'that goes on within the soul, since it takes greater delight if things that it loves are found or restored to it than if it had always possessed them?' Augustine proceeds to mention a victorious general who experiences the greatest satisfaction when the danger is greatest, a seafarer who exults in calm

*seas after a violent storm, and a sick man who upon recovery walks with a joy he had never known before his illness. **'Everywhere a greater joy is preceded by a greater suffering.'** "*

—PHILIP YANCEY, *Where Is God When It Hurts?*

(quoting and paraphrasing Augustine from *The Confessions of St. Augustine*)

It's incredibly clear that our times of disappointment are meant to draw us closer to God, to help us to understand our desperate need for the Savior He sent. His desire is to create a greater faith, a deeper love, and an unshakable trust to carry you through the journey. All the while, His loving hands hold you up and reassure you that He will never leave. He surrounds you with His unfailing love and embraces you continually with His grace. God has an eternal purpose for allowing you to go through every trial that you face. He wastes nothing... *especially pain.* You can be confident in His promises:

So do not throw away this confident trust in the Lord. Remember the great reward it brings you!

(HEBREWS 10:35 NLT)

Trials of life take their toll, tragedies can bring us to our knees, and disappointment can linger indefinitely, but through Christ *we can face everything* that comes our way, knowing that there is an eternal reason for the circumstances in our lives. We must go to God in prayer and ask Him to help us *respond* correctly, *receive* His love through the pain, and *remain* strong in our faith—we must trust Him *completely*.

We must be determined to fight the good fight of faith (see 1 Timothy 6:12), trust that His ways are higher, and grasp the fact that they are also *better*. Hold fast: God's love prevails.

> "To those going through the valley and shadow of death, hear this word: Weeping will last through some dark, awful nights—and in the darkness you will soon hear the Father whisper, 'I am with you. I cannot tell you why right now, but one day it will all make sense. You will see it was all part of my plan. It was no accident. It was no failure on your part. Hold fast. Let me embrace you in your hour of pain.'
>
> "Beloved, God has never failed to act but in goodness and love. When all means fail—his love prevails. Hold fast to your faith. Stand fast in his Word. There is no other hope in this world."
>
> —DAVID WILKERSON, *When All Means Fail*
>
> *(His last words, which he posted on his blog on the morning that he was tragically and suddenly killed in a car accident. Truly, our loss and heaven's gain.)*

Know this: Trusting God will cost you *something*. It may be pride, selfishness, wrong attitudes, addictions, lust for life, or whatever else keeps you from being in the right relationship with Him. But there is a divine exchange—in return . . . you get peace.

CHERIE HILL

*May the God of hope **fill you***
with all joy and peace as you trust in him,
so that you may overflow with hope
by the power of the Holy Spirit.

(ROMANS 15:13 NIV)

4

Perfect Peace

Thank you Father, for peace that surpasses all

e long for it more than anything else, though our souls will rarely recognize it. Our spirit yearns but rarely obtains what we need the most—*peace*. Through our trials and tribulations, our souls are pushed and pulled between the *very little* we know and the *great unknowns* of life. If we'll stop long enough to listen, God's silence is calling us—from the mountaintop, where He stands waiting for us. He wants to give us a glimpse of the valley from a different vantage point.

We're looking for Him to speak and act through a windstorm that sweeps away our fears, or by shaking our world and putting things into place.

Perhaps it would be fitting for Him to appear in a fire from heaven that consumes our pain and suffering, leaving us with peace. *But it doesn't happen that way.* Amid all the chaos, He *whispers*.

"Go out and stand before me on the mountain,"
the Lord told him. And as Elijah stood there,
the LORD passed by, and a mighty windstorm hit
the mountain. It was such a terrible blast that
the rocks were torn loose, but the LORD was
not in the wind. After the wind there was an earthquake,
but the LORD was not in the earthquake. And after the
earthquake there was a fire,
but the LORD was not in the fire.
And after the fire there was the sound of
a gentle whisper.
(1 KINGS 19:11–12 NLT)

Life is unpredictable—so is God. (Although as you get to know His ways, His overall plan is always the same: redemption and refinement.)

In the midst of job loss, terminal illness, broken relationships, and fear of the unexpected, God wants to give us peace. Instead of the thing we want, He gives us what we need—*supernatural tranquillity that is unchanging through our valleys of life.*

The peace that God gives is not as the world gives. It's not happiness. *We go looking for peace in all the wrong places.* We think we've found it, only to lose it again. When we're walking in darkness, we have no hope of having any peace at all.

They have not learned
the path to peace.
(ROMANS 3:17 ISV)

Through our pursuit of God, we stumble across a path...a path to peace. But it wasn't the way we were expecting to go. We had determined our own way through this life, yet God is leading us quite another. Once again, God shows us the way and leaves the decision to us.

We've come to a fork in the road along our journey and we must trust in His ways and realize that He never leads us anywhere that He cannot keep us. If He's leading us into a valley, He'll walk with us and provide all that we need to make it through. He not only wants us to take this journey with Him through valleys of adversity, but He wants us to experience His peace *through* it.

This path to peace comes through trusting Him. It's being content with not knowing exactly what will happen in the future, but trusting God to take care of us no matter what lies ahead. The exchange, once again, is divine—we surrender fear and anxiety and He gives us peace.

But it's not that easy, is it? We need to know. We reason that if we just knew what our future held, we'd be able to have some peace in life. We'd be able to settle our hearts and minds and focus on the present. Yet deep down, we know it doesn't work that way, and so does God.

He emphatically commands us not to lean on our own understanding. It's far too limited. His ways are far better than ours. Whatever we can devise *doesn't even compare* to His will.

Trust in the LORD
with all your heart

*and lean not on
your own understanding;
in all your ways submit to him,
and he will make your paths straight.
Do not be wise in your own eyes.*
(PROVERBS 3:5–7 NIV)

Reasoning, struggling, and trying to figure out everything in life will steal your peace. We must stop trying to figure out God and how He will work everything out in our lives... in order to have peace, *we have to stop worrying.*

Winning Over Worry

It's been said, *"Worry is like a rocking chair: it will give you something to do, but it won't get you anywhere."* Worry can get the best of us. It consumes our lives and leaves us continually desperate and hopeless. Here's the truth about worry (according to various psychological studies):

40 percent of our worries are about events that will never happen,

30 percent of our worries are about events that have already happened,

22 percent of our worries are about trivial events,

4 percent of our worries are about events we cannot change, and

*4 percent of our worries are about real events on which
we can act.*

So the bottom line is that 96 percent of what we worry about... *we have no control over.* That equates to wasted time. And we simply don't have time to waste in this life. With that in mind, we need to remind ourselves of the truth about worry—worry has NEVER solved a problem.

Jesus asked an interesting question:

*Can all your worries
add a single moment to your life?*
(MATTHEW 6:27 NLT)

It's a question that begs an answer in each of our lives. And the answer is obviously rhetorical. We must realize that Jesus isn't trying to insult us by asking such a ridiculous question... *He asked it to convict our hearts and turn us toward God.* He asked because our worrying is taking us in the wrong direction—in the sight of God, worry is a sin. It's a sin because the root of our worrying is unbelief. And as hard as that is to accept, it is truth. Just take a look at Jesus's words in Matthew 6:25 (NIV):

*"Therefore I tell you, **do not** worry about your life, what
you will eat or drink; or about your body,
what you will wear. Is not life more than food,
and the body more than clothes?"*

His command is no different from those of the Ten Commandments. "Do not" are strong words. There's no

need for interpretation. There's no chance of *misinterpretation*. And if God tells us not to do something…it is with good reason. Our worrying is clear evidence of our lack of faith in Him. If we're trusting in God completely…there should never be a need to worry. We hear Jesus's words pierce through our sin once more in Matthew 6:28–30 (NLT):

> *"Look at the lilies of the field and how they grow. They*
> *don't work or make their clothing…*
> *And if God cares so wonderfully for wildflowers that are*
> *here today and thrown into the fire tomorrow,*
> *he will certainly care for you.*
> ***Why do you have so little faith?"***

His words, at first, seem condemning, but in reality, they are freeing. Through those words, Jesus is telling us some things that are profound and powerful to our lives. *He's showing us the way to peace.*

First and foremost, we must recognize worry as a sin. We need to continually confess our sins. We can have no peace while we are harboring unconfessed sin. Jesus commands us not to worry three times in verses 25, 31, and 34 of Matthew, chapter 6, so that means worrying is being disobedient to God. He's telling us we don't have to worry. *We have a choice.* He's showing us that we can take responsibility for our sin and turn from it. If we'll confess our sin of worry, God will give us peace that will guard our hearts and minds. And that's what we need. Peace that will protect us from the chaos of life.

Do not worry about anything;
instead pray about everything.
Tell God what you need,
and thank Him for all He has done.
Then you will experience God's peace,
which exceeds anything we can understand.
His peace will guard your hearts and minds as you live in
Christ Jesus.
(PHILIPPIANS 4:6–7 NLT)

Instead of worrying, we're commanded to pray. It's when we pray, when we seek God and His promises, we learn that we CAN trust Him. If we say we believe, *then we must live as though we do.* We must trust God instead of living like He doesn't exist. You see, worry is not the root of our problem... *our lack of faith is.* Our worry is a denial of God's love, power, and wisdom. As hard as it is to accept, in God's great love and wisdom, He's brought us to the very place where we are crying out for mercy. In times of doubt and despair, when worry gets the best of us, we can cling to God's promises that will not return void.

"It is the same with my word.
*I send it out, and it **always** produces fruit.*
It will accomplish all I want it to,
and it will prosper everywhere I send it."
(ISAIAH 55:11 NLT)

God has given us incredible promises on which to build the foundation of our lives, yet we tend to "*lean unto*

our own understanding, instead of trusting God with all of our hearts." Amid the crises of our lives, we give in to worry.

Though we rarely feel as though our prayers are even making it to the gates of heaven, we tend to keep praying…but we forget to start *praising*. Praise turns our doubt to faith and eliminates the worry. Our praise says, "God has accomplished it." Praise tells God that we worship Him for who He is, not just what He gives. We can't praise Him and worry at the same time. We have to learn to step aside and believe that God can accomplish more in our lives than we ever can. We need to give Him the benefit of the doubt and realize He more than likely knows what He's doing. If He's working, *then we can rest.*

> "Come to me, all you who are weary
> and burdened, and I will give you rest."
> (Matthew 11:28 NIV)

Rest, that's what we desperately need. We need to stop trying and simply start *trusting*.

> God can always handle what we can't. We can trust Him fully, and rest in Him completely. Worry only moves us into the direction of doubt, And doubt will never take us where only faith can. So, it's in our doubt that we have an opportunity to believe what we might not otherwise.

> Instead of worrying, we must surrender it all to God, over and over, until we rest from trying and simply start trusting.
> —Cherie Hill

"Today is the tomorrow we worried about yesterday."
—AUTHOR UNKNOWN

"For peace of mind, resign as general manager of the universe."
—AUTHOR UNKNOWN

"Don't be afraid of tomorrow, for God is already there."
—AUTHOR UNKNOWN

We can say all we want about worry...worry still tends to get the best of us. But there's a reason. *We have an enemy.* And the moment you declare your trust in God, he'll show up at your front doorstep, eager to come inside...often he'll barge right in—*an uninvited guest.*

Know Your Enemy

Your enemy is not a person, the circumstances of your life, or God; your enemy is Satan himself. The sooner you acknowledge his existence, the sooner you'll be able to fight in the battlefield of faith—the *real battle.* Like it or not, you're in a battle for your soul. But *it's not flesh and blood you're up against.* Your battle is with spiritual forces in a heavenly realm.

> *For our struggle is not against flesh and blood, but against the rulers, against the authorities, against the powers of*

this dark world and against spiritual forces of evil in heavenly realms.
(EPHESIANS 6:12 NIV)

Each time you make the decision to trust God in your life, you will find the devil knocking at your door. You might assume he'd devour you in weakness...*but he pays no attention to those who are his*; he's interested in those who are a threat to his power. If you've developed unshakable faith, you can be certain the enemy is going to try and shake you.

He knows that it's by faith that God's power is released, souls are saved, and every promise of God is obtained. He knows that when we surrender to the Lord, our weakness turns to strength and we become courageous in the battle. "*By faith, righteousness is born and demonic fires are quenched....Simply put, faith sustains those who possess it,*" David Wilkerson said.

We're warned throughout Scripture of our enemy and how he works. We're alerted that in the battle of faith, we will be tempted to cast aside our faith. When life gets hard and the battle grows intense...we'll be tempted to leave the path of truth and *go our own way.*

*They have left the **path of truth**.*
(2 TIMOTHY 2:18 NLT)

The enemy approaches your faith subtly. He begins to speak lies of defeat into your life and then convinces you that there is no hope. He's out to destroy your faith because you've set your heart on truly trusting the Lord. So instead of making himself obvious, he knows it's wise to invite you for a cup of coffee to chat awhile. (He doesn't want to make his tactics too obvious.) The conversation seems reasonable, as he even *appears* to make sense.

He'll try to convince you that there is no way out of your situation... that things are going from bad to worse and *you* have to do *something*. "Besides," he says, "*You've waited long enough on God and He just isn't showing up.*" He goes on to show you that you just don't possess enough faith to get you through your valley. In a moment of truth, you recall the words of Jesus:

> "I tell you the truth, if you had faith even as small as a mustard seed, you could say to this mountain, 'Move from here to there,' and it would move. Nothing would be impossible."
>
> (MATTHEW 17:20 NLT)

Someone's lying. But the enemy asks, "Well, has the mountain moved?" It's hard to argue with that when you're still in financial distress, your child has only days to live in the hospital, or your spouse continues to travel a road of addictions. In fact, it seems the devil knows what he's talking about—*God isn't showing up.*

As he sees he's got your attention, he takes his tactics one step further and poses the idea that it's actually *God* who is causing your heartache. He asks aloud, "What

kind of loving God allows you to go through the pain and suffering you're going through?" Then, in your silence, he starts to bring to your mind all of the Christians who have claimed to trust God but who suffer terrible tragedies, sickness, and even death. He grabs at your weakness that he senses and candidly asks, "What makes you think that God is going to answer *your* prayers?" Now he *knows* he's got you. So *he offers you a deal.*

He convinces you that you are suffering unjustly and that he alone can fix it all for you—if you'll just walk with him awhile...he'll prove it to you. He'll show you the way of escape. You'll find peace, though temporary. *His short-term plan is a long-term tragedy.* Yet you'll never know it, until that sad day when you realize *you've been lied to*:

> "... there is no truth in him.
> When he lies, it is consistent with his character;
> for he is a liar and the father of lies."
> (JOHN 8:44 NLT)

When our pain and suffering are prolonged and our soul grows weary, we're easily persuaded by the devil's lies. He works to keep us hopeless and steal our peace and joy. The enemy comes into our lives for good reason—to steal, kill, and destroy.

> *The thief's purpose is to steal and kill and destroy.*
> (JOHN 10:10 NLT)

If he can't steal your joy, and your salvation is sealed, then he'll work diligently to kill and destroy your peace. He prowls around in your life, just waiting to devour you.

> Be alert and of sober mind. Your enemy the devil prowls around like a roaring lion looking for someone to devour. Resist him, standing firm in the faith…And the God of all grace, who called you to his eternal glory in Christ, after you have suffered a little while, will himself restore you and make you strong, firm and steadfast.
>
> (1 PETER 5:8–10 NIV)

The truth is that we're told many times in Scripture that we *will* suffer. There will be trials and tribulations in this life (see John 16:33). Yet in Christ we are MORE than conquerors (see Romans 8:37). The *rewards* of trusting Him far outweigh the *risks*. We must hold on to truth at all times, in order to withstand the attacks of the enemy. And although we may fight him off for a time, we can be certain he'll return at a more opportune moment:

> When the devil had finished tempting Jesus, he left him until the next opportunity came.
>
> (LUKE 4:13 NLT)

Be ready. Know truth so you can detect the lies. When you grow weary in the battle, rely on Christ's strength…, *not your own.*

While the enemy is in pursuit of you, you must be in pursuit of peace.

Let him turn away from evil…
*seek peace and **pursue** it.*
(1 PETER 3:11 ESV)

By Faith

Our foundation of all peace is our faith in God. Our peace *with* God and *in* God is found only by our faith *in* Christ.

"Let not your heart be troubled:
you believe in God, believe also in Me."
(JOHN 14:1 NKJV)

If we don't have peace, then what we know in our heads has not made it to our hearts. If we don't have peace, we must pursue Jesus…it's Jesus that holds the key to our peace.

It is through our faith in His life, death, and resurrection that we have our peace with God. Through our peace with God, we find the *true* peace we need to persevere through *any* circumstance.

"Peace I leave with you; my peace I give you. I do not give
to you as the world gives. Do not let your hearts be trou-
bled and do not be afraid."
(JOHN 14:27 NIV)

When we have peace, we have no fear. When we fear God, *we have no reason to fear anything else.* If we fear only the Lord, He will keep us safe (see Isaiah 8:12–14). True peace comes from Christ alone. As we learn to trust in God's word on how to experience His peace, we come to understand that *by faith* we believe that God is sovereign, He loves us unconditionally, He works all things for good, and He is a ready help in times of trouble.

Through our surrender, we find unshakable peace—peace that is unflinching and unwavering. When we're experiencing true peace through our faith in God, we're content and steadfast and we're anxious for nothing. If we trust in God, we find that the peace that rules in our hearts can calm any of life's storms.

> *"To trust in spite of the look of being forsaken; to keep crying out into the vast, whence comes no returning voice, and where seems no hearing; to see the machinery of the world pauselessly grinding on as if self-moved, caring for no life, nor shifting a hairbreadth for all entreaty, and yet believe that God is awake and utterly loving; to desire nothing but what comes meant for us from His hand; to wait patiently, ready to die of hunger, fearing only lest faith should fail—such is the victory that overcometh the world, such is faith indeed."*
> —GEORGE MACDONALD

His peace can carry us through any valley. In every circumstance, God's peace through His grace proves to be

enough. We must be committed to casting every care into His hands, trusting that He alone will handle it best. We must continually *choose* to trust God, *even when there appears to be no evidence that we should.* Faith doesn't walk by sight, but trusts God at His word and walks forward with confidence and assured hope. And "*when we don't understand... when we can't see His plan... when we can't trace His hand... we can trust His heart.*"

A Heart for God
Deborah Ann Belka

A heart that is peaceful,
knows in God it can trust
it knows believing this
is a daily must.

A heart that is satisfied,
knows God is always there
it knows it can give Him
its every worry and care.

A heart that is content,
knows God is good
it knows He will do
just what He should.

A heart that is committed,
knows God always leads
it knows He will supply
all of its wants and needs.

A heart that is devoted,
knows God loves its praise
it knows He is faithful
and follows all of His ways.

A heart that is for God,
can never go wrong . . .
for the heart that loves Him
is steadfast and strong!

Quite frankly, we may never understand even *parts* of His plan. Only rarely do we see His fingerprints from day to day or His faithful footprints in the sands of life. Most often, we can only know His ways *through trusting His heart*. And in the end, it is God alone who will keep you in perfect and constant peace.

> *You keep him in perfect peace whose mind is stayed on you, because he trusts in you.*
> (ISAIAH 26:3 ESV)

In our darkest hour, when it seems as though the sun will never rise, we must never quit crying out to the Lord.

Your faith in God says that you believe in Him more than you believe in your job loss, your divorce, your addicted spouse, or your cancer. If you're not delivered *from* your thorn, you'll be delivered *through* it. If He doesn't change your circumstances, He'll change you to be more like Christ . . . and THAT is a miracle! We must be assured through our faith that when God allows, brings,

or orchestrates circumstances in our lives, regardless of the relationships, influences, factors, and decisions involved, God knows about every single possible scenario. God tracks all the implications of all that happens in you, through you, and around you. *He is sovereign.*

God has *His ways.* We might not think they are better, *but they are.* We might not think He knows what He's doing, *but He does.* Our problem is that we're looking for a quick spiritual *transaction* that gives us what we want, instead of a spiritual *transformation* that reaches into eternity.

We have a "God On Demand" mentality: we want Him around when we need him, but would like Him to stay out of the way the rest of the time. You see, it's our difficulties, our valleys, our storms of life that reveal what kind of faith and hope we have. God wants to work within us, because if we'll let Him, He knows the joys that are in store for us in the end. And remember: everything will work out in the end . . . if it's not working out, *it's not the end.*

> I consider that our present sufferings are not worth comparing with the glory that will be revealed in us.
> (ROMANS 8:18 NIV)

If you're walking with God, the journey isn't over just because you hit a bump in the road and get a flat tire. The story of your life is still being written, but when you're trusting in Jesus, if you're letting Him write, you're assured a far different ending than any you were ever expecting.

*Let us…fix our eyes on Jesus, the pioneer and perfecter of
our faith. For the joy set before him he endured the cross,
scorning its shame, and sat down at the right hand of the
throne of God.*
(HEBREWS 12:1–2 NIV)

The truth is, when it comes to trusting God, there are no
easy answers. In fact, sometimes, *there are no answers at all.*

I called him but he did not answer.
(SONG OF SOLOMON 5:6 NIV)

But sometimes God wants *us living within our unanswered
questions.* Sometimes He simply wants us waiting, hoping,
and praying. The *silent* Savior is also the one who *saves.*

As we resolve to the fact that God is in control, we also
grasp that although things may get better, they also may get
much worse. We wonder how long the pain will last…and
we don't know. We wonder why we're going through such
devastating storms of life…and *there is not an answer.* We
want to know if God is with us…*finally* we have a reply:

*And surely **I am with you always**,
to the very end of the age.*
(MATTHEW 28:20 NIV)

As we seek a God who loves us and yearns to be gracious to
us, we must trust that through His love, one day our faith will
win over doubt…light will break through darkness…and
love will defeat all else and everything in between—one day
we will see our Redeemer face-to-face (see Job 19:25).

Though we can't understand His ways *entirely*, we can trust in them completely.

Faith doesn't require us to understand, it only demands that we trust.
—CHERIE HILL

If you're stuck in a place where your heart is just not realizing what your head understands, ask yourself this question:

"What would you do if you were absolutely confident God was with you?" ···
—PETE WILSON, *Plan B*

[handwritten note: ask this how I can / what I can do to prepare me / purpose / what is my purpose you will for my life?]

In times of affliction, when your faith is struggling through the doubt, stop to receive and believe in the love your Heavenly Father has for you. Accept it as truth instead of believing all the lies. He has calmed greater waters than yours. He's brought down higher mountains than the ones that stand before you.

In the valley of your life, God is proving your faith—not for Him, *but for you*. You need to know where you stand with God—it's vital. Though we cry out for one more sign, one more miracle, one more word to get us through... God, in His silence, is teaching us to trust Him in ways we never thought we could or would.

Let me prove, I pray thee, but this once with the fleece.
(JUDGES 6:39 KJV)

There are degrees to our faith. In the beginning of our walk with God, we aren't concerned with our spiritual growth... *we just want signs and miracles.* Like Gideon (see Judges 6), we give God tests. At times God gives us what we need in order to grow our faith in *this way*; at other times, when He doesn't, He's telling us that we're ready to move on in our faith. He's moving us from an infantile stage into a more mature faith. If He leaves us where we are now, our faith will be imperfect... and He's promised to perfect our faith, *remember*? (You read that promise only three pages ago... see Hebrews 12:2.)

We're always looking for a feeling from God, some token of Him besides His word. We can know that we are walking stronger in our faith and closer with the Lord when we trust Him... *without any evidence that we should.*

When the mountains aren't moving, when the giant still stands before us—ready to take us down—and when the Jordan River is at flood stage with no way to cross into the Promised Land... faith and trust in God gives us the strength to take the next step, even when all human reason urges us to the contrary.

Once again, Paul shows us how to trust God, regardless of what we see. He urges us to walk by faith and *not by sight.*

The terrible storm raged for many days, blotting out the sun and the stars, until at last all hope was gone.
(ACTS 27:20 NLT)

In the midst of fear and uncertainty, Paul rose up to encourage the others:

> So keep up your courage, men, for I have faith in God that
> it will be exactly as he told me.
> (ACTS 27:25 NIV)

Paul wasn't holding on to his circumstances, He was holding on to God. He trusted Him...and so must we. There is no other way for the mountain to move, the seas to be parted, the giants to be taken down, or the raging storm to be calmed. All other ways will be proven a failure in the long term. It's God's way or our own... *it's our choice.* It's when all hope seems gone that God is giving our faith the opportunity to infinitely grow. Take that chance... *you won't regret it.*

> When is the time to trust?
> Is it when all is calm,
> When waves the victor's palm,
> And life is one glad psalm
> Of joy and praise?
> Nay! But the time to trust
> Is when the waves beat high,
> When storm clouds fill the sky,
> And prayer is one long cry,
> O help and save!
>
> When is the time to trust?
> Is it when friends are true?
> Is it when comforts woo,

And in all we say and do
We meet but praise?
Nay! But the time to trust
Is when we stand alone,
And summer birds have flown,
And every prop is gone,
All else but God.
What is the time to trust?
Is it some future day,
*When you have tried **your way***
And learned to trust and pray
By bitter woe?
Nay! But the time to trust
Is in this moment's need,
Poor, broken, bruised reed!
Poor, troubled soul, make speed
To trust thy God.

What is the time to trust?
Is it when hopes beat high,
When sunshine gilds the sky,
And joy and ecstasy
Fill all the heart?
Nay! But the time to trust
Is when our joy is fled,
When sorrow bows the head,
And all is cold and dead,
All else but God.

—L. B. COWMAN, *Streams in the Desert*

Trust that He is for you, even when everything appears to be coming against you (see Romans 8:31). Never stop praying and crying out to God, even when it seems that He's not listening—*He is*. And when you can't seem to find any hope, encourage yourself with the promises that He's made to you. God hasn't made ONE promise He won't keep.

> *Turn my eyes from looking at worthless things; and give me life in your ways ["your word"—(NIV)].*
> (PSALM 119:37 ESV)

> *This is my comfort in my affliction, that Your word has revived me.*
> (PSALM 119:50 NASB)

It is God who will make *your way* perfect, if you'll trust in *His ways*. When there is no other hope in this world, when you're at wits' end and your world is falling apart at the seams...trust God—***no matter what***.

> *But blessed are those who trust in the LORD and have made the LORD their hope and confidence.*
> (JEREMIAH 17:7 NLT)

Scripture Promises to Encourage Your Faith

God is our refuge and strength,
A very present help in trouble.
Therefore *we will not fear,*
though the earth should change
And though the mountains
slip into the heart of the sea;
Though its waters roar *and* foam,
Though the mountains quake
at its swelling pride.
There is a river whose streams
make glad the city of God,
The holy dwelling places of the Most High.
God is in the midst of her, *she will not be moved*;
God will help her when morning dawns...
He raised His voice, the earth melted.

The Lord of hosts is with us;
The God of Jacob is our stronghold.
(PSALM 46:1–7 NASB)

It is God who arms me with strength
and keeps my way secure.
(2 SAMUEL 22:33 NIV)

The Lord gives strength to his people;
the Lord blesses his people with peace.
(PSALM 29:11 NIV)

Blessed are those *whose strength is in you,*
whose hearts are set on pilgrimage.
(PSALM 84:5 NIV)

He is not afraid of bad news,
his heart is firm, trusting in the Lord.
(PSALM 112:7 ESV)

When they hurled insults at him, he did not retaliate;
when he suffered, he made no threats.
Instead, *he entrusted himself*
to him who judges justly.
(1 PETER 2:23 NIV)

"This is my command—be strong and courageous!
Do not be afraid or discouraged.
For the Lord your God is with you
wherever you go."
(JOSHUA 1:9 NLT)

Now all glory to God, who is able,
through his mighty power at work within us,
**to accomplish infinitely more
than we might ask or think**.

(EPHESIANS 3:20 NLT)

Show me your ways, LORD,
teach me your paths.
Guide me in your truth and teach me,
for you are God my Savior,
and **my hope is in you all day long.**

(PSALM 25:4–5 NIV)

In his kindness God called you to share in his eternal
glory by means of Christ Jesus. So after
you have suffered a little while, **he will
restore, support, and strengthen you,
and he will place you on a firm foundation**.
All power to him forever and ever! Amen.

(1 PETER 5:10–11 NLT)

In quietness and **confidence**
is your strength.

(ISAIAH 30:15 NLT)

So humble yourselves under
the mighty power of God,
and at the right time he will lift you up in honor.
Give all your worries and cares to God,
for he cares about you.

(1 PETER 5:6–7 NLT)

Let all that I am wait quietly before God,
for *my hope is in him*.

(PSALM 62:5 NLT)

Be glad for all God is planning for you.
Be patient in trouble, and **always be prayerful**.

(ROMANS 12:12 NLT)

About the Author

Cherie Hill is the founder of Scripture Now.com, a global ministry that brings the blessing of Scripture to more than thirty countries. Cherie takes joy in helping others explore the promises and blessings found within God's Word. She has a BA in psychology and biblical counseling training through the American Association of Christian Counselors; she writes for several online Christian magazines and counsels through various radio programs. When not writing or speaking, she commits her time to her church and to various nonprofit organizations.

Books by Cherie Hill

Waiting On God

Hope Being Gone

When You Need a Miracle: Seven Secrets of Faith

Be Still: Let Jesus Calm Your Storms

Beginning at The End: Finding God When Your World Falls Apart

empty: Living Full of Faith When Life Drains You Dry

Faith Under Construction

His Love Never Quits: Finding Purpose Through Your Pain

ggf ♡♡♡

GGF ♡♡♡

GGF ♡♡♡

GGF ♡♡♡

5.23.17
? ??
2015~?
2016?
was in box ~
Journal for
Sept. 2014
When did I place
this book?